'*Adventures in a Foreign Land* is a [...] mental illness but of faith. Lo[...] concern and passion about the ef[...] mental illness as she has experienced them, [...] between and with golden thread, her journey of faith. Through the pages of the book she offers to fellow sufferers and carers a credible companionship and story of hope; and to the Church, a compendium of insights and guidance which will assist faith communities in creating safe space for those experiencing mental health difficulties. The book is a testimony of the author's courage as she continues to adventure in what has probably become a less foreign and more familiar land for her. It will hopefully encourage and inspire those who feel they are in uncharted territory.'
Teresa Onions, former Pastoral Leader of St Thomas Church and former Director of Pastoral Care UK

'This is not, as you might imagine, an account of distant travels, but rather a very honest account of someone who has struggled deeply with mental illness , in particular bipolar affective disorder.

'She describes in detail the phases of her illness, firstly when she was in a manic phase and then her struggles with the recurring depressive phases of this illness. She points out the necessity and benefits of medical treatment and is open about the familial aspects of this illness.

'She is also a firm believer in the power of prayer and finds God's help in a very real way in her difficulties. She learns to be patient with herself during recovery and to pace herself as she takes on her previous responsibilities. She also found great peace in nature.

'Strengthened by her experiences, she began to move out towards others and worked with her church to set up a group for those struggling with mental health problems. Impressively, this group continued for twelve years and many people were helped by it. The group was well and carefully set up, and this wisdom was further demonstrated in her involvement with carers of those with mental illness.

'I believe this book will be very helpful for those who go through similar mental health problems. I also believe it will be a useful resource for carers and others helping those with mental health problems. It also shows how mental health services and church groups can work together for the benefit of individual sufferers. I highly recommend this book.'

Dr Stephen Critchlow, retired consultant psychiatrist and church pastor, and author of Mindful of the Light

'I am so pleased Lorraine has shared her experiences of mental illness and of supporting people through their struggles with the wider world.

'I was a member of the MHF and through the group I learned not to feel guilty about my mental health issues and found a place where I could be value to others. Our MHF meetings were the highlight of my week; we supported each other and were guided and encouraged by Lorraine's leadership.

'I commend this book to anyone seeking to build an inclusive Christian family.'

Frances Price, a member of the Mental Health Fellowship (MHF) for ten years

Adventures *in a* foreign land

*Discovering Jesus' compassion
for the mentally ill*

Lorraine Gibbard

instant
apostle

First published in Great Britain in 2018

Instant Apostle
The Barn
1 Watford House Lane
Watford
Herts
WD17 1BJ

British Library Cataloguing-in-Publication Data

A catalogue record for this book is available from the British Library

This book and all other Instant Apostle books are available from
Instant Apostle:

Website: www.instantapostle.com
E-mail: info@instantapostle.com

ISBN 978-1-909728-84-4

Printed in Great Britain

Acknowledgements

My grateful thanks and love to my husband, Ian, who has shared the adventure and is my best friend. To our beautiful girls, always an inspiration and our joy. To Maureen, who encouraged me to write, and to Christine and Anne, kindred spirits who listen and love. Thanks also to the family of believers in my church, to Teresa, Alison, Christine and Frances for their help and for the members of the Mental Health Fellowship who have taught me so much.

My most grateful thanks to the Lord, who can reach into those dark places in our lives and bring His steadfast light, love and healing.

Contents

Introduction

My intended readership includes those experiencing mental distress now, those who have suffered in the past and those who care for them.

While I am not a health professional, I am someone who has experienced the reality of living with mental illness.

I developed bipolar disorder shortly after I became a Christian, and I learned to manage and achieve good mental health within the safe harbour of Jesus' guidance and love.

Mental ill health can be experienced by famous people, artists, sports personalities, writers and actors. Fame and money do not act as barriers. This foreign land can claim many souls.

People can hide mental health problems, and for many that is because they are afraid of the judgement of those around them. Any hidden problem can encourage shame to grow. If we pray for God's light to shine in these places, shame has nowhere to hide. Education and training can raise awareness of mental health needs, and this can do much to alleviate the ignorance and fear, which often travel together, and the prejudice that can develop from both.

The Church forms the front line of God's response to a hurting world. Where better to learn how to support those with mental health issues? I began to see God's vision for our church develop in a mental health support group. The family of the church began to show greater awareness, acceptance and understanding of mental health issues.

In this book you will find strategies outlined which have helped me cope with bipolar disorder. I also describe how I have used my insight into mental health issues when supporting others who experience them.

I draw from thirteen years' experience of working in churches and I pray that this book will have something to say to those with an interest in letting the light into this hidden area of mental distress.

Beginning

When I was younger, I knew very little about mental health issues, and I did not know anyone who suffered from depression. All my information came from newspaper articles telling of mad axemen who had slaughtered innocent victims and how the insane had been imprisoned in psychiatric institutions. This was a foreign world and nothing to do with me. But now I have walked in that foreign land and I have gained a very different perspective. It has taken long years of reflection, healing and growing to come to this space in time where I can begin to face the challenge of putting into words what I have learned, and be prepared to face any stigma that comes my way because of it.

I was born in the tiny hamlet of Walkeringham in County Lindsey. This was a county which bordered South Yorkshire, Lincolnshire and Nottinghamshire. They redrew the county boundaries in 1974 and my birth county became no more. We moved many times in my early childhood and so I had no understanding of a permanent place to call home.

As I grew, my family did settle into a more permanent home and we began attending church. It was while listening to the Sermon on the Mount when I was eight years old that I first recognised who Jesus was. The hairs stood up on the back of my neck and I became convicted of the truth and power of God's Word. I began to see how right it was that God was central in our lives. Unfortunately my family stopped going to church, and being too young to go by myself, I reluctantly stopped going too. I continued to read the Bible and pray, but I did not know any other person who wanted to share this with me and I felt lost in the hugeness of this mission.

When I was eighteen years old tragedy came to my family. My dad died very suddenly one night after suffering from a heart attack. I was deeply shocked and heartbroken. I had lost my best friend and my protector; I felt alone, abandoned by the one person who had always been there for me. This marked the end of my childhood.

All my siblings felt an instinct to protect Mum from our pain, and her total brokenness made it impossible to speak of my trauma to her. I was furious with God, because He could have stopped Dad from dying, but as I directed my rage at Him in secret, shedding my first adult tears, instead of being offended He graciously gave me a picture. This was the first time I had ever had a picture come to my mind like this. It was of a crossroads. I looked down each path and knew I did not have the courage to go down them alone. I realised my need of my heavenly Father more powerfully now that I had lost my earthly father.

I often think of that picture whenever I read a favourite verse in Jeremiah: 'Stand at the crossroads and look; ask for the ancient paths, ask where the good way is, and walk in it' (Jeremiah 6:16). I was aware that God was in my life, but I did not really understand that He wanted a close personal relationship with me every day. It took more years and experiences of God to bring me to a defining moment.

I went to Liverpool to teacher training college one month after my dad died. No one knew I was grieving. This was a new start for me, so I grieved with God at night. One night I had the most vivid dream, of Dad and heaven; it comforted me and this was my first 'God dream'. I was to discover that these dreams never fade and they always have a powerful message.

I flourished in Liverpool, enjoying life to the full. I became involved with the Christian Union and went to church occasionally. Towards the end of my student days a 'God incident' – where I was not expected to get into a housing scheme, yet despite all odds, I did – was instrumental in my meeting a young architecture student who was to become my husband. Looking back at those days once I had become a Christian, it seemed as though God was looking after me even before I had really committed my life to Him, or understood what it meant to truly follow Him. Our wedding day was a great joy and the feeling of blessing as we exchanged our vows was very powerful. We had three children, and each one brought such gratitude into our hearts we felt the need to say 'thank You' to someone.

Our families put pressure on us to have the children christened, which in turn challenged Ian and me to think about making a commitment to a church. We knew we did not want to go and say promises we did not mean and then never go to church again, as we had seen others do. So we chose a church and became involved in its life. There was much to hear and learn. We saw Christians living out their faith, being real and yet brave and generous.

In this loving community of believers, I became hungry for a deeper experience of God. I saw others who had the assurance of God's love for them, and I wanted that. I began to study the Bible and testimonies, enlarging my knowledge of God and the story of His people. I was reading a book called *Holy Fire* by Colin Urquhart,[1] which instructed me to go to the cross, confessing and repenting of my sin.

I knew I had come to a place of life-changing decision and that I wanted to be different, but how would I feel if I went to the cross and nothing changed? I remember feeling as if I was on a precipice and could not go back nor stay where I was – so I stepped off.

I chose to go to the cross, and as I brought each sin my heart became more sensitive. I began to feel how my sin hurt Jesus, and started to cry. I could see how my sin separated us, and the pain of it was terrible. I recognised that my heart was breaking, because this was as intense a pain as I had experienced when my dad died. As I wept, something caught my focus. A light in the sky was moving towards me; it seemed to be actually dancing as it came to me. The light had warmth and it came to pause over my head. I was still and my weeping had stopped. I could barely breathe as I waited.

Slowly the presence of this light came into me and slowly moved down my body; a feeling of great and deep

---

[1] Colin Urquhart, *Holy Fire* (London: Hodder & Stoughton, 1984).

peace began to replace the pain and anguish of moments before, and as I waited for what would happen next, fluttering movements began in my stomach and what felt like bubbles began to rise; this developed into the most powerful joy I had ever experienced.

My mind was forming a truth, which I would repeat many times: 'Jesus is alive and it's all true.' Now I know to call this presence the Holy Spirit, but this first time all I could do was gladly experience His acceptance, love, peace and joy.

My understanding of what Jesus had done for me was very clear at that moment. I was still feeling the aftershocks of His actions in my life. Jesus had chosen to go to the cross, not for His sins, but for mine. He had taken upon Himself the punishment I deserved.

I remembered hearing a children's story when I was eight years old about a lion who chose to be a sinless sacrifice, and died in place of a traitor. That story of Narnia had resonated in my heart. I had thought how wonderful it was to have someone so brave, selfless and loving who was prepared to die instead of an undeserving traitor.

Then I realised I was a traitor. I had been disobedient, rebellious and faithless to God. Then I thought of something else. You cannot betray someone's trust unless they believe in you. It made me gasp to realise God trusted me, and that each time I failed to maintain truth in my life, or was negative or unkind, I was not fulfilling the principles of that heavenly country I was part of. I asked God to help me to be obedient. I did not want to turn against Him.

As I thought through all of this, I began to realise that my value to God was very high. Could I have given my daughters as a sacrifice for others? God the Father had done this for me. My life had new significance, new purpose and new power, which I felt surging through me. I was living a new life because Jesus had died in my place.

I had looked upon the cross as Jesus was crucified in films and acknowledged the awful suffering, but had not known the power of what He achieved. How amazing that the Son of God took on such a rescue mission for the whole world – that that one perfect sacrifice should stand for all time. Only Jesus could do this, the only one fully human – and so able to die in our place – and fully divine – able to live in this world without sin – could be that sinless sacrifice.

I now knew that through Jesus' death and resurrection, I had been given a way to die to sin and be raised to new life. How could I say 'thank You' for such a gift? Love was indeed stronger than death (see Song of Solomon 8:6)!

I had been afraid that Jesus would not want me, and was astounded and delighted to find that He did! I was elated and so full of joy that friends and family noticed the change in me. I was bolder and full of energy, with the love and confidence to reach out to others. I also felt a profound sense of belonging, which was new for a woman who had always longed to belong and never really achieved it outside of her immediate family.

I saw how Jesus had drawn me to Him because of my need to belong. In church I felt accepted and loved by people I admired; suddenly I was part of a worldwide family. I had been baptised in the Holy Spirit. I longed for my husband to meet with the Holy Spirit too and be changed by Him, and I prayed for this to happen.

I was a full-time mum with three small children, and did not have much time on my own. I became creative at finding time to be with the Lord, and He repaid me by graciously feeding this baby with spiritual milk. I asked Him to help me to learn and understand the Bible, and He gave me a hunger for His Word and a gift of remembering it for myself and others. I was eager to learn from God and He was so close and I knew that He accepted me exactly as I was, and was intimately involved in all of my life. My prayer life grew because my trust in God grew with each answered prayer.

Life was exciting and sweet. I was convicted of the need to write down the 'God incidences' which were flowing through my days. I knew they were important and did not want to forget anything, so I began my first spiritual journal. I also tried to capture my new and deeper experiences of God, but words were not adequate. I found myself lost in praise and prayer. I began to have experiences of God's pain as I prayed, and found myself weeping for the lost or the suffering.

My husband was watching me carefully, wondering about this new person he was married to. I had prayed for him constantly, that he would receive a gift of faith, and I had talked with him about God's Word. Friends from church were also being helpful and lovingly inviting him into their lives.

As I prayed for my husband's salvation, with great passion, God gave me a picture of our family sitting around the dining table saying grace, and I took this as a promise. Ian received Jesus into his life three months after the experience I mentioned above – when I had been baptised with the Holy Spirit. The day Ian said yes to Jesus I saw a vision realised, as we all sat round the dinner table, held hands and said grace together as a family. Sometimes there are no words to express our love of God and our gratitude to Him. My husband became a Christian just at the time I really needed him to. God's timing is perfect.

Looking back over the thirty-five years I had lived without knowing God closely, I saw evidence of his guardianship, guiding me through tragedy and bereavement. I was not fully aware of the protection He gave, but I knew someone was guarding me. Now I was in His light, and entirely His, yet the echo of those lost years would make me sad sometimes.

I had often cried as the Holy Spirit came to me. I wondered why this happened, and thought that it was as I encountered His perfection in contrast to my imperfection that I felt remorse and this found expression in tears. The tenderness I felt, which came after the tears, was very different. I tried to capture my feelings in a poem.

I Love You

I love You with all the intensity of my
Hungry, questing soul.
Like a child reaching trusting arms high to You
With the gratitude of a turbulent heart's first
Kiss of peace.
I love You with an artist's joy at the sight of a
Rainbow in a dark sky.

I love You with wonder and certainty that you can
And do love me.
With every good thing in this child's life
You are worshipped, honoured and adored.

As the poem formed in my mind I quickly wrote it down. This was my first experience of God working through me in this way. It was cathartic, and I was amazed at how empowering writing down such ideas was. It was soon joined by other poems. They would come in the darker times and the agitated times. They became my voice to express all that I had been through, and my way of trying to make sense and learn from it.

One night I had a dream. I was sitting on a knee looking out at the world, and I was stroking His beard with my fingers. The profound peace I felt and the safety, acceptance and belonging were very strong. I fought to stay in the dream as I woke, so as not to leave that powerful feeling of contentment and delicious sweetness. I so enjoyed this feeling of being perfectly at home, as if for the first time. Even so I was shocked that I could dream that I sat on God's knee. Later I tried to find out what the disturbing and wonderful dream had meant.

Jennifer Rees Larcombe in her book, *Journey into God's Heart: The True Story of a Life of Faith*,[2] spoke of the Hebrew 'To seek the Lord's face or enquire of the Lord' which she explained could just as easily be translated as 'To stroke the Lord's beard'. I did not know this at the time, but that is just what I was doing, wanting to know the Lord, even in

---

[2] Jennifer Rees Larcombe, *Journey into God's Heart: The True Story of a Life of Faith* (London: Hodder & Stoughton, 2006).

my sleep. I thought nothing would be able to take away the joy of knowing where I truly belonged.

Years later I wrote about this dream in a poem.

Promise

I still remember the intensity of that waking
    moment
The slow release from such piercing sweetness
As I came back to consciousness I clung as
A new baby instinctively, to the fading beauty.

I was astonished to be allowed so close
Overshadowed by Old Testament warnings
Yet my spirit recognised that complete peace,
Knowing protection, acceptance and love.

I wondered at my ability to dream like this,
Yet my soul knew a belonging, which overcame fear
I had never known before in waking, the perfect
    peace
I knew as I was cradled in the arms of my Maker.

This is a promise I stand on; when in alien
    surroundings
When life is hard, when even among friends I feel
    alone,
I remember that this life is transient, one day we
    will go home
The promise fulfilled, will be so much more than we
    can imagine now.

There was a feeling of euphoria in me and an activeness and excitement, which was new. We all welcomed it because I was very happy, confident and outgoing. There was an eagerness to respond to every demand made on me.

I became involved in many projects. I felt like I had the ability to do anything, so I did. My thoughts were rapid and very intense; every aspect of my life I would put under rigorous scrutiny. Being too busy to sleep, I read and prayed in the early morning, and if my thoughts did get a little confused or frightening I would pray them away.

I did get impatient with the slowness of others, and I found it difficult to wait for them, as I was already racing ahead to the next thought. I experienced deep emotional intensity and my natural restraint was gone. I could be rude to strangers I did not like and had the ability to cause a scene without feeling inhibited. Yet I was intensely happy most of the time.

I had a phrase to describe my compulsive following of one word and letting a train of thought take me off in any direction. 'Catherine Wheel' thoughts are explored in this poem. I found it hard to fully capture the menace and brittle brilliance of these experiences.

Too Early

Catherine Wheel thoughts ignited by sparklers in
   my brain
Shoot off to all points of the compass.
Any thought patterns, which remain
I chase along the fine thought web
Until I am stranded on a far-flung outpost.

Confused, I wonder why I am here
I call plaintively for home.
Now rushing back along the thought trails
Another spark attracts me.

Tirelessly I pursue with skill and energy until
A clamouring of offensive noise strikes my ears.
Sensing danger I rein in my thoughts,
It's morning, but much too early for it to be
Time to get up and face another day.

Slowly I began to believe that people were plotting against me, that they were using codes to try to fool me. I could see connections everywhere, and my mind became like a web, endlessly making connections with people and situations. My thoughts were getting disjointed and it disturbed me, but I explained it away and concentrated on the good things. Reality began to blur for me. I was obsessed with my own thought-life, and losing discernment and judgement.

As mania increased I became more expansive, bold, and always creatively, tirelessly reaching out to others. Reading my spiritual journal from those days I can see how the entries of that time changed quite suddenly from ordered recordings to long lists of incoherent collections of thoughts, without useful conclusions. Even the writing itself changed; I began to use a pencil, and the script was large and untidy with many crossings-out. Just looking at those pages now brings concern and sadness for the person who wrote them.

My confusion became intense and because I was a new Christian who had felt very close to God, and was experiencing many new and challenging stimuli, separating the facts from my mind's fantasy was very difficult. When I tried to read the Bible, the words danced in front of my eyes, and whenever anyone tried to confront me I would argue against them, believing I was right. Reason was drowning in the pressure of swirling ideas.

I was very tired. I needed to iron the children's clothes, but somehow I could not focus or concentrate. I remember feeling as if I was on a roller coaster, but it did not stop. There was a feeling of danger and isolation in these days, and I stopped sleeping. I did not realise it then, but my behaviour was considered bizarre, even by those who loved me. My GP said she was concerned, but I felt I knew better and ignored her advice.

I was sectioned under Section 2 for assessment and 3 for treatment of the 1983 Mental Health Act[3] and forcibly taken into a psychiatric unit. This meant I could be detained and treated for up to three months without my consent. I was traumatised as surely as if I had been in a roller coaster crash.

The only way I could trust what these strangers in white coats were saying, was that Ian had allowed them to take me away. I trusted his love and protection and knew that if he was part of this incredible happening, I must truly be ill.

The Victorian building I was incarcerated in was gothic in reality and in my experience. They had padded cells and very few home comforts. To walk those corridors at night

---

[3] 1983 Mental Health Act. Open Government Licence v 3.0, http://legislation.gov.uk (accessed 29th November 2017).

because I could not sleep, was one of the low points of my life. There was not even any escape in sleep from the bewildering, overwhelming challenge which was my waking experience.

When I was first diagnosed with bipolar affective disorder I was manic, delusional and paranoid. I had lost control of my mind; it no longer worked in any useful way. I thought in codes, often turning the usual meaning of a situation upside down. Nurses were out to kill me and not to be trusted. I was not informed about my illness, treatment, or my medication in those early days. I felt disenfranchised and a non-person. It was only as I began to exert my independence that I started to receive some information, but that was some time later.

Mania was a strange driving force, a destroyer. My mind took me to wild and terrifying imaginings until the drugs I was given took away my ability to think at all. My will, my thoughts and my actions went into a fog of nothingness. I was exhausted, physically, mentally and emotionally.

The days were without hope and my anguish was difficult to bear. God spoke to me then and said, 'Remember these things.' I was not sure then, but I felt He was telling me that He could use my experiences in some way.

Mania went from me and the hole it left was filled with grey numbness. Thoughts began to form again, but my emotions were hibernating. This was cruel; after the trauma of mania, I needed to feel God's comfort. But I felt as if I was in a vacuum. It was hard to wait and hold on in faith when all I had to help me was the memory of what had gone on before.

I chose to believe that God was with me right then, but how I wanted to feel His presence and to know His joy. I waited for Him; indeed, I could do nothing else. Dressing was beyond me; sitting still, impossible. I shook from morning to night. I lost the ability to listen or speak. I could not focus without great effort. I felt trapped in my own mind. My thoughts felt unstructured and vulnerable, and my soul was tortured.

As I began to look back at all that I had experienced since coming into the psychiatric unit, it felt like a bizarre, unending nightmare. One night I gave up the struggle to live, and sought an escape. As if on autopilot, I was steered away from danger by strong arms and into the path of a nurse. I did not see my rescuer, but I believe when I was helpless and hopeless and felt that I was of no earthly good, God sent help in my gravest hour of need. 'For he will command his angels concerning you to guard you in all your ways; they will lift you up in their hands, so that you will not strike your foot against a stone' (Psalm 91:11-12).

It was months later as I read this psalm that I knew the truth of God's provision for me. I knew in hindsight that God had saved me by sending His Holy Spirit to heal my mind, had provided medication and a safe place in the hospital, and had sent His people to comfort and accept me; and an angel came at just the right time to save me. God saved me in every way.

This song expresses what I experienced.

> To the lost Christ shows his face
> To the unloved he gives his embrace

To those who cry in pain or disgrace
Christ makes, with his friends, a touching place.[4]

I learned that when no human reaching out can touch you, the Holy Spirit comes and takes up residence, quietly, gently shielding the most vulnerable wounds, and abides with you, closer than breathing. I was aware of several reassuring touches of healing, which eventually not only healed my mind and body, but also healed my emotions and spirit. This verse from Psalm 10 (verse 14) expresses what I knew to be true:

But you, God, see the trouble of the afflicted;
you consider their grief and take it in hand.
The victims commit themselves to you;
you are the helper of the fatherless.

It was amazing to me as I read Isaiah 63:9: 'In all their distress he too was distressed, and the angel of his presence saved them.' God cared for me and what I was experiencing; He felt my pain and responded.

Yet it was now that I learned the truth that faith is not an easy gift to unwrap. I developed my faith muscles in the 'gymnasium of depression', an expression used by Dr John Lockley in his work on depression.[5] Using fingertip faith, I clung onto what I knew of God.

---

[4] John L Bell and Graham Maule. Extract from 'A Touching Place', copyright© 1989. Iona Community. 21 Carlton Court, Glasgow G5 9JP. Used with permission.
[5] Dr John Lockley, *A Practical Workbook for the Depressed Christian* (Milton Keynes: Authentic, 2002).

I waited for my experience of God as I had known Him, but He did not turn up. So knowing that He did love me, and hoping that He was not a capricious God, I waited. Those were hard days and they stretched my faith muscles until they hurt. Having loved God, there was no way I would accept life without Him, so I kept on waiting. I still find waiting the hardest thing to do!

Visitors who came to hospital were of two types. Those who cared for me as I was, and who brought love and humour with them, but no stresses of the outside world. Others who came felt the need to talk about anything, to cover their nervousness of being in a psychiatric unit. The information they gave me of the world I neither wanted nor needed. They tired me out long before they went. In my emotionally vulnerable state, I could sense their unease. I did not have the strength to help them, so just needed them to go.

One visitor to hospital was eagerly anticipated. I was very thankful to God for my husband, who already had insight into caring for someone who had special needs in his family. He seemed to know I could not take in the details of life back at home and so protected me. He covered for me, waiting patiently for me to return to myself.

As I made progress I was allowed 'leave of absence' from the unit. This meant on some evenings he would collect me, as if on a date, and we would sit in a quiet public house and talk of our children, holidays and other hopeful things. Those 'dates' were so important.

It took a long time to come away from the fearsome land I had been walking in. The sadness of knowing I could not look after our children, the acceptance of my diagnosis, the trauma of it all and the numbness of depression... A depressive episode can be the opposite end of the mental health pendulum from mania. In exhaustion you feel helpless, there is no self-confidence or motivation, and you doubt everything.

I delayed getting up in the morning because it took energy and some decision-making – very demanding things to achieve – and once up I had to connect with a world that frightened me. There was a grey blanket over me, which filtered out the colour, warmth and vitality and all positive feelings. Dread, fear and self-loathing were my companions.

My days were unstructured and time seemed to stand still. I was miserable, trying to occupy myself in order to make it move faster. Walks were on offer, but only when certain nurses were available to accompany you.

Reading was not a useful activity, as I could not see the written words on the page; they danced in front of me. When I forced myself to see them, they would not stay in my mind. This took all my effort and gave me no joy.

One thing I did manage to do was knit. In the lounge of the unit was the biggest roll of knitting I had ever seen. Patients would pick it up, knit as long as they wanted, and then put it down again. This sample of knitting was a record of achievement. The varied stitches and colours made a glorious sort of scarf, which rolled down the stairs and would have gone to the next floor if not retrieved by a nurse. What a communal activity.

Another activity I was encouraged to do was colouring. It did force me to focus on one thing and to persevere. I focused so hard on staying within shapes with the crayons that I forgot my pain for a while and it absorbed some time.

We also had appointments with the psychiatric nurses, where we had discussions about life now and where we wanted to go from here. We all decided that a 'normal' state is subjective. One person's normal is another person's abnormal.

We had one other planned activity. Pottery class was held on Friday afternoons. This brought a fresh character into our week, a calm, pleasant man who offered us another opportunity of passing time. It could be therapeutic as we worked the clay and produced finished works of art. I felt like a child taking her work home as I displayed it to my admiring family.

During dark times, you must choose how you respond; you can become bitter and resentful, or you can follow the Spirit's leading and learn from your suffering. Accepting what is helps you to move to new levels of dependence on God. This may not be easy and you may have to change, but you may also learn more of who God is and how He wants you to go on with your life.

I spent hours listening to God, trying to read His Word, resting and waiting. After many months I did begin to feel the gentle stirrings of a wish to start my life again. When I cried out to God, asking why He had allowed all of this suffering, He said, 'In this crucible of suffering I am forging a healer.' I was not convinced I had heard correctly, but I let it settle in my heart.

I knew what it was to be ignorant about mental health issues. Before my illness, I had been unaware of the pain of such things and that the harmful attitudes of others would only increase the pain. So my education began in an under-resourced Victorian hospital ward. I was given no information in hospital so I did my own research. As I mentioned above, leave of absence was given from hospital. With each leave you managed, more leave was granted. These times were hard, as you were discovering for yourself just how much you could achieve. I felt so weak and any external stress became unbearable for me. I'm so grateful that I was blessed with a capable and loving husband who protected me and three adorable children who behaved so gently with their broken mummy. As I surmounted basic challenges like driving the car or doing a supermarket shop, my confidence grew. My care for our children became a precious thing, which I gloried in.

Back in hospital after leaves of absence I listened to the other patients in my ward. Some were institutionalised by their condition. Thoughts of a life other than this were never spoken of. That chilled me – would I become like this? Others were fearful, as they had experienced stigma from many different people. One lady spoke of neighbours watching her guardedly, behind net curtains, making her feel ashamed, and so she was dreading going back home.

I examined my feelings and wondered what my extended family would say. There was a mixed reaction. One was horrified that I was in a place 'like that' – she meant the psychiatric hospital where I was receiving care – but most wanted to comfort and help as much as they could. My mum marched down the long hospital corridor and, although I knew she was uncomfortable, brought normality with her.

My husband was a constant source of love, strength and understanding, and our children gave me motivation and determination. Our church family served us and prayed for us and accepted me back into church with great care and love.

After the Storm

So it was that I came back into my life from being somewhere else. How did I feel when I was finally discharged from hospital? Eager to be home, wanting to pick up on life again, to reclaim what the bipolar had stolen, but wary of going too fast. I had learned that for me, too little restraint could be deadly.

One thing this terrible illness had given me was perspective. I had no energy to waste on what the world considered important if it was not in line with what God considered important. My sense of identity was deeply bound up with my relationships, first with God and then with my beautiful family.

It was my GP who first gave my illness a label, and although hard to face the diagnosis, it was the beginning of accepting and owning bipolar. I taught myself about the illness, learning to understand the symptoms and the boundaries of this huge burden. My doctor helped me to become familiar with the medication I was on and fostered confidence in me as I learned to use it to meet my own particular needs. The term 'expert patient' used in long-term illness to describe the patient who could monitor the effects of medication and outside stimuli better than the professionals, encouraged me to take charge of my care.

An elder in my church prayed with me and helped me to emotionally accept the need for ongoing medication by describing it as just one of the resources Jesus provides, and encouraged me to accept it as a personal gift from the Lord.

One thing I would like to have done was talk through my loss of health, and the struggle to find out who I was now, with a counsellor, who could have listened objectively and not been burdened as family and friends would be. This was not available to me. I felt unheard on many occasions and unsupported.

Occasionally I would have disturbing memories come to me from my time in the psychiatric unit. One way of dealing with them was to give them to Jesus and command them to go away. Another helpful method was to write about them. This helped me to process what I had experienced.

I remember during mania experiencing a frightening vision. When I looked at ordinary scenes, I interpreted them differently; they were far from normal. I would sometimes see the same phenomenon in other patients. I attempted to catch this in words.

Diamonds in Their Eyes

Who are these people who enter here?
Through the doorway of entrapment
Their eyes glisten as if they see
Through diamond eyes.

They look through shards of glistening glass,
Giving them distorted, untrue vision.

They believe what they see because for now
It is all they know of truth.

I know what it is to see through fractured eyes
Where only glimmers of truth show through.
Yet the colours glow and flash as light catches
The many lenses which refract colour.

As medication begins to work
They will find the shades fade.
Their lenses flatten out and refocus
Sight begins to come back to normal.

For a time the world may seem monotone
Perhaps it is their contrast setting out of kilter
But over healing time they may find another
Kinder, truer vision, which will bring hope.

There were times when I missed the feelings of euphoria, of confidence and energy. Now I was cautious, hesitant, and many warned me to go slowly. I was still weak and easily tired. Getting used to the side effects of medication took time for me. Gradually my mental health and emotional well-being improved, but I was troubled because I did not know how to measure the amount of work I could do or commitment I could safely give. I had been brought up in a family that valued hard work; my slower pace of life was challenging to my self-esteem.

The pattern of my life became a steady rhythm of looking after our children, taking space to be with God and slowly taking up roles in our church.

I grew in confidence in my parenting skills, and began to trust my ability to balance the demands of life and stay well. There were times when I had to say no to requests to help in church, which was hard to do. I felt some judged me, but I knew what was more important. The choice to be wise with what God had given me or to overcommit and risk relapse was no choice at all. I never wanted to experience mania again.

This did not mean that I did not have battles still to fight. Making decisions could be difficult. Sometimes I still felt out of sync with the world, and this felt like an ache in my bones. Depression was a closer threat to me than mania. I needed to have the faith to believe that my life would be useful, and that joy would return.

As I pondered on a way in which I could increase my workload without taking risks, God gave me a picture of an old set of scales. The balancing weights would allow me to see if the output of energy needed for each new task depleted me, or if I could healthily maintain that level. So by considering one task at a time I would accept new work, and then assess how I felt with this new burden, before going on with more. It was a slow way forward, but it worked for me.

I lacked the opportunity of knowing other bipolar sufferers, especially Christian ones. I knew of a bipolar support group, but the timing was wrong. I was not emotionally robust enough to take on other people's pain alongside my own. So I remained isolated in some ways. I longed for the right person to come alongside me who would understand without words my needs, my pain. The

Holy Spirit did that, but I still longed for human understanding.

There was a wistfulness in me and a hesitation to trust my emotions as I began to know a feeling of warmth in my heart again after a long absence. I prayed for God's guidance and decided to trust Him. I wrote this as I tried to move on.

Waking

I am waking from the longest most terrible sleep
Drowsy, still struggling with the ties that bound me
Dare I hope that I am free from this nightmare?
Has this living fear come to an end?

The dream feels more real than the waking world.
This transition state is confusing.
How do I go on from here? Show me, Lord.

I am still troubled by what is behind me
Yet I can feel a gentling in my soul
I no longer feel like that person I was before,
So who is the me that will go on from this waking?

My moods would fluctuate, and I knew I must be mindful of my vulnerability. I was extremely sensitive to other people's moods too, and this could become a burden to me. I would be exhausted by other people's demands and expectations.

I learned to recognise the warning signs as the protective mechanism began to work. I instinctively closed down my willingness to process the needs of others. I met the needs of our children, but I would not give out energy I did not have. My husband and I would change roles once he was home from work. He would take over caring for our children and I would do the household chores. This enabled me to mentally and emotionally switch off.

When I felt like this, going out in the open air would always help. Now it is well-known that exercise encourages serotonin production and release, and that this brain chemical in the right levels helps stabilise and elevate mood. I did not know that then, but I did know walking helped me.

My favourite place was a stretch of the riverbank local to us. The steady flow of the water seemed to soothe me. Agitation would go and I could think more calmly. The timelessness of the river spoke to me of God's provision and His permanence in my life.

Nature continued to have the power to pacify me, and the next spring, our family went on a picnic to a local beauty spot. I have always loved bluebells. They bring back happy childhood memories, and the colour and fragrance have always held a particular charm for me. To my delight there was a bluebell wood, and we had a great time exploring it. I was so moved by the experience I recorded it in this poem.

Bluebell Heaven

There it was, boldly and proudly proclaimed.
Bluebell Heaven, up the hill on the left,
I trudged upwards, already weary but lured by the
Promise.

I was tired from months of chronic illness, but as I
Became committed to my quest, my steps became
Surer.

A trickle of bluebells marked the boundary and I
Drew breath as the scent grew stronger.
Then suddenly, there, before my incredulous eyes
Lay a blue haze which carpeted the contours of the
Hillside.

In every direction was a sea of swaying bells.
The blue intensity drew tears as I began to believe
The beauty I saw. Reverently I wandered.
Thanking God for this sumptuous feast for the senses.

Sweet fragrance soothed my spirit as I savoured
This peace. My heart was full.
Fatigue began to melt away as joy took its place.

Bluebells are fragile, delicate emblems
Sent by the God who loves to heal.
The tranquility of this lovely glade
Made me glad to be alive
A message from heaven was here in the bluebells.

Holidays were great times of escape for me. Outside of
usual commitments, I had time to just 'be'. One joy was to
walk by the sea and dream. When I could, I would choose
to walk alone along the seashore, the sea lapping at my
ankles, and allow myself time to gaze in wonder at God's
creation.

I remember one such walk; the rocks at this particular
spot were banded in different coloured layers. Each rock

had responded differently to the weather. The bottom layer of rock was compact and hard and deep red. In contrast, the next honey-coloured layer was open textured with attractive honeycomb holes. Other layers had rust colours threading their way through them. All different, yet the effect was harmonious. It struck me afresh that there is a plan for all creation, and all we need to do is be ourselves, each of us beautiful and useful in our own way.

I acknowledged that this illness, which had robbed me of my life in some ways, had given me new gifts. Once I had started to recover, I did so with new eyes. Things became clearer, and I was aware of things I had not been aware of before.

It took time to grow in confidence in managing my various medications, and it also took time to work out how to monitor my reactions to differing situations. My GP warned me to be sensible and not to expose myself to too many stimuli. But I wondered if by living so cautiously I was restricting my openness to God.

It was approaching Christmas, so many activities were on offer for my children, and I felt torn and sad. How did I 'do' Christmas in a way that was good for us all? It was the first anniversary of the onset of my illness and I was feeling pensive.

I was reading and praying by myself when the Lord answered my prayer in an amazing way. He spoke my name in a loud, audible voice. I was so shocked I looked around the empty room, but even as His voice reverberated I recognised Him. He called my name and reminded me of the joy He had given me. His use of my name reassured me that my name is in the book of life (see Revelation 13:8; 21:27).

I believe the Lord spoke to me in an audible voice because if my mind had received the words quietly by the Holy Spirit, I'm not sure I would have been able to accept it, remembering how ill I had been a few months before. This direct and entirely supernatural way of reaching me broke through my fear and blessed me profoundly. 'Joy, Lorraine' was no hopeful suggestion, it is and will be so. How like Him to choose a way of reaching me that even I could not doubt!

I thought of Isaiah 43 where a beautiful, intimate picture of God's love for His children is drawn. That passage has remained a favourite for me. God knowing my name and claiming me for His own answered a question I had not dared ask. Was this illness punishment for something I had done? Did He no longer love me?

Chapter 9 of John's Gospel tells us of a healing of a man born blind. His disciples asked Jesus, who sinned – his parents or the man himself? Jesus said neither sinned, but this happened so that the work of God could be seen in his life. Illness is not punishment, and nothing will ever separate us from God's love (see Romans 8:38-39).

One thing which became a priority for me was time alone with God. When I neglected that I became vulnerable – I grew anxious and sad. My medication made it difficult to be alert in the morning, and trying to read the Bible was a real labour of love.

My challenge was to get the children to school, nursery and toddler group. I learned to be flexible when organising my time so I could be quiet with God. If our toddler needed a nap, the nurturing side of me wanted to do housework and food preparations, but the natural side of me wanted to sit down in a quiet room and listen to God.

Martha and Mary, the two sisters beloved by Jesus, have often battled it out in my mind. I liked it best when Mary won, and so did my family (see Luke 10:38-42). Somehow the family meals were produced, and the house was cleaned.

The Lord had given me a hunger for His Word, as if to make up for the years I had not read the Bible. I was reading the story of Abraham and Sarah and came to Genesis 22, where Abraham is told by God to sacrifice his own son. I was so shocked, as I read on, to see how Abraham obeyed God completely even when it would break his heart, and he did not understand why he was being called to do this terrible act.

It took the angel of the Lord's intervention to stop Abraham from carrying out the instruction. Abraham had passed the test, and would forever be an example of unquestioning obedience to God. But I was angry; had the Lord not known how difficult this was for Abraham? Why had He done this? Then insight came. Abraham trusted God so much that he would do whatever He asked, trusting in God's love and faithfulness. He had been spared this awful sacrifice. But God had sent his only Son to earth to become a once-for-all perfect sacrifice for all our sin. Jesus was not spared, and neither was Father God. They both went through with Jesus' crucifixion. God knew the pain of allowing His only Son to die in our place. I realised that God does not ask us to do anything that He has not done first. He knows very well what it can cost us to do difficult things in order to be obedient to Him. He could never be indifferent to our pain, because we were bought at such a great price and are infinitely precious to God.

Relapse did come; even as I experimented with the perimeters of my mental health, some unexpected trouble would flair. I noticed depression come on me suddenly, and as I wondered what had contributed to this, I acknowledged my fear – why now? I was dismayed with the speed my mood had lowered and that I was not aware of any particular thing which had caused it.

As I walked home after leaving the children at school, a poem formed in my mind, and I quickly wrote it down.

Relapse

I know this place
I've been here before
The clutter of lives
Breaking my strength
No one hears my silent scream
Few can perceive my pain
I struggle to hold my life in balance

The threads of the web are too taut
I know the tension is wrong
There is nothing I can do
The pieces of my life disintegrate
I call out as I free fall down

'What can I hold on to, where is my fixing point?'
And Jesus replies, 'You hold on to Me'
His hand grasps mine and I cling to His.
Healing begins again.

Capturing on paper how I felt was so helpful, and clarified things in my mind. I was grateful to Jesus for direction and reassurance.

Pride can be a problem when you realise you are so dependent on Jesus, and yet who better to depend on? His strength never fails. I prayed for healing many times, but although I was healed emotionally and spiritually and my self-worth increased, the illness stayed. I became very grateful to God that once I had learned to manage my medication, and adapt my approach to life, I was well most of the time.

I would probably always have a weakness, but I knew I was in good company. The apostle Paul wrote about his 'thorn in the flesh' which he asked God to take away. God's reply to Paul was, 'My grace is sufficient for you, for my power is made perfect in weakness' (2 Corinthians 12:9). We learn to trust others slowly as we depend on them and they do not let us down. When we depend on God for our lives on a daily basis, we can find out just how much He loves us and will keep His promises. God feels very close when you need Him this much.

I was growing in my spiritual experiences: learning the power of meditating on God's Word, and the joy of speaking and singing in tongues, and I felt the call to pray.

The gift of tongues that God had given me was not easily claimed. There were reports in the early Church of disciples speaking in different languages they had not learned, and this was as soon as they had been baptised in the Holy Spirit at Pentecost. This had not happened to me. I was hesitant to accept the gift of tongues as I did not understand it.

It was while I was away on a retreat that I first encountered people singing in tongues in an evening meeting. The sound was heavenly. As I closed my eyes and listened, my spirit knew that this singing was of God. My trust in this gift soared, and I wanted to receive it for myself.

I looked to the Bible for evidence of this gift: 'to another miraculous powers, to another prophecy, to another distinguishing between spirits, to another speaking in different kinds of tongues, and to still another the interpretation of tongues. All these are the work of one and the same Spirit, and he distributes them to each one, just as he determines' (1 Corinthians 12:10-11). It was while I was taking part in an Alpha course in our church that an elder prayed for me to receive the gift of tongues. I was making strange sounds, but it wasn't until I dared to speak out loud that I was convinced I had received this gift. And so I accepted it as a gift for me, and began to practise it.

Now, as I used tongues, I found it released me to praise more freely, and in prayer, to pray when I could not find the words. After singing in tongues, I always felt a stronger connection with God; it helped me (as it promises in 1 Corinthians 14:4) and it helped people I was praying with to be edified.

I had experienced the power of prayer dramatically in my own life and now I wanted to pray for others. My husband and I were asked to lead a home group and all these experiences were helpful in our care of the people in it. We were eager to learn and grow in faith and the home group became a wonderful part of our lives.

As I looked back over the last few years where so much had happened, I found myself writing again. This poem traced my changing relationship with Jesus through those years.

Deeper

When I met Jesus I saw His perfection and all my
　　sin
The gap between us was an agony to my soul.
I wept as only the broken can, with nothing held
　　back
I was in complete surrender.

Jesus' spirit cleansed me and quieted me,
His joy was born in me for the first time.
The afterglow bathed my world in a golden light.
Life was sweet, vibrant and exciting.

I could not wait to be with Him.
Breathing His spirit deeply in.
Amazed at His acceptance of me.
Glorying in the new insights into His truth every
　　day.

I became aware of paddling in the shallows
As Jesus called me to go deeper.
I lived for the joy of Him and His great love,
Daring to follow as He called.

Illness came like a tidal wave,
Knocking me off my feet and under,
Into the maelstrom of pain and fear.
'Why me, why now?'

I discovered deeper secrets in that dirty beige
    hospital ward,
That Jesus is faithful, that no place is off-limits to
    Him
However horrible or forbidding it may seem.
He can save His friends from hell on earth with
    great power
And gently and gradually teach them a new way to
    live.

Painfully I acknowledged that my perception of
    Jesus
Had been shallow. There was so much more to
    learn.
My love must go deeper, as I go deeper into Him.

I read in my journal from the previous month how I had
been struggling to maintain my equilibrium. I had been
nudged into an unsettled period of depression because of
changing life experiences, but I had taken my weakness to
the Lord. I had learned how to use medication to help and
submitted everything to Jesus. I had not struggled in my
own strength, but had rested in the Lord's strength.

I experienced depression on a yearly basis. October
seemed to be the month; it was uncanny. Every year a
relative in my extended family would die and the funeral
would be an ordeal. While I was busy I coped, but once I
was home again my strength would fail and my mood, like
the weather, would become grey. I became skilled at
putting on a coping face, but once the children were at
school I would slow down each day and rest and pray.

It took so much energy climbing out of depression each year that I went to my GP. I said, 'I don't want to spend the rest of my life on an emotional roller coaster ride.' She suggested I went on a low-level maintenance antidepressant, which I reluctantly agreed to. I still found it difficult to be faced with this diagnosis of bipolar; to absorb the realisation that I was dependent on medication for life was another huge challenge.

Now I was taking mood stabilisers and antidepressants. The stigma attached to both in our society was well-documented and expressed openly. Shame could have set in, but Jesus continued to make His love clear to me, and our church family made their acceptance known. I was very grateful for the Lord's provision for me.

A Vision to Grow Into

As I grew stronger I began to piece together evidence for this illness from my past.

I recall feeling anxious at bedtime one night. My older sister, who usually shared our bedroom, did not come to bed. My routine of settling down for the night was disturbed and, as I waited, I became more unsettled.

I remember closing my eyes and trying to go to sleep. It seemed that the more I tried, the less sleep would come. As I lay in the dark, I began to feel pulsating sensations within my head, and throbbing sounds. I became aware of the systems of my body working and moving. Suddenly there was a shooting beam of light and a screeching noise. I opened my eyes to a dark, quiet room.

I felt frightened and alarmed; my heart was beating fast and my mouth was dry. I did not know why I had experienced this. It was so beyond anything I had known before. I felt very alone. I did not understand what was happening and even less, *why* it was happening. As a child I could not find the words to describe what I had experienced, and so I did not share it with anyone.

This happened to me over the years, haphazardly. I did not know when it would come.

My CPN (community psychiatric nurse) who visited me after I was discharged from hospital encouraged me to talk about my experiences. One day I did try to tell him what had happened to me as a child, and most recently during a weekend stay at home from hospital, which had become tense. He told me I had described an experience others had endured, but struggled to express. His appreciation of my account encouraged me to wonder if I had a way of helping others to know that they are not alone in this, that they are not the only ones. He validated my story and I felt for the first time that something good could come from this.

The Lord was leading me to learn more about mental health issues, and kept providing opportunities where I could explore ideas and find answers to questions. I had a deep longing to meet someone else who suffered from bipolar. I needed to share with someone who understood, without my having to try to explain, the fear and excitement of extreme mood swings; to share the constant need to find balance, and to hear what they did about that in their own life.

A friend persuaded me to go to a Christian woman's conference. During a time of prayer we were encouraged to pray for someone we did not know. My friend went one way and I went another. She soon came back with a lady and suggested I pray with her.

This lady suffered from bipolar and her child was also a sufferer. As I listened to her I felt a flow of empathy, and I knew this was a very significant meeting that God had brought about. I asked the Holy Spirit to give me the words to pray. She was burdened with guilt about passing on the propensity for this illness, and my heart longed for her to

52

be free. It seemed as if we were flooded with light as I prayed; I cannot remember the words clearly, but the effect was peace and healing for both of us. We both felt a powerful connection in our shared experiences.

I marvelled at the way God had brought the two of us together. I was in a distant city, there were many people in that hall, yet my friend had brought this lady to me, and something beautiful had happened. My longing to meet a fellow sufferer had been fulfilled, but my desire to meet others grew. The quality of the sharing of two sufferers in that moment sparked a desire in my heart. I wanted to be able to meet other people with bipolar so we could share experiences and faith and be stronger together than apart. I began to pray consistently for that to happen.

I visited my uncle after I had returned to family life. I was fascinated as he talked. It was as if my vulnerable mental health had given him permission to speak. He had never spoken like this before and no one else in the family ever had. He spoke naturally of an older family member going 'high', becoming expansive in thought and speech, making ill-considered decisions and putting himself in danger at times. He confirmed my suspicion that another child in my generation also suffered from manic depression, or bipolar affective disorder as we now know it. I honoured him for his candour and for giving me such rare jewels of information.

I was so grateful to my uncle and so dismayed that no one else had ever told me about our genetic inheritance. It felt like there was a conspiracy of silence. Was this to protect the person who was ill, or protect the family from the stigma of having a family member with bipolar?

Perhaps no one felt they could speak with understanding? They did not want to look too closely at an uncomfortable area of family life? Or did they hope it was nothing to do with them, presuming it would not be part of their inheritance?

These revelations made me wonder how other families responded to the news of their loved ones' mental ill health and how this affected their acceptance, caring for and living with the consequences of that person's mental distress. How many families keep secrets about vulnerable members, and why?

I remembered the fellow patients I listened to during my hospital stay; some of them had shared fears about the prospect of going home and facing neighbours and family. They knew from previous experience that judgemental, critical attitudes would probably be there for them to endure again.

Something welled up in me at the cruelty and injustice some people had received. I did not know what I could do about it; indeed, I was not strong enough to know where to begin, so I asked the Lord what He felt about it.

The issue of guilt is powerful for those struggling with the matter of their genetic passing on of illness. There is evidence as in my family that bipolar, like many other illnesses, runs in families. The fundamentals of the illness are locked into who you are. It felt cruel that I had no way of changing this. There is a fear that once you have learned the propensity of the illness in your family, you may always anticipate it in your children. This can become harmful as the fear simmers in your mind. When I prayed about this, the Lord reminded me that He was in charge in my life, and I gave Him my fear and prayed for a cutting off of that genetic link with our daughters.

I began to understand about perfect love casting out fear (see 1 John 4:18). Our children have shown no signs of inheriting the illness, and I pray fervently that this will continue. I wrote a poem asking more questions than suggesting answers.

Guilty?

I passed it on, the illness, which blights me
The one thing I did not want to bequeath.
My beloved one, whom I dreamed of,
Prayed over and loved, suffers too.

Why has this happened, when I prayed
That this would not be?
How do I bear a pain so overwhelming?
What good can come from this?

I did not choose this
Nor can I change it
So tell me, am I guilty?
No crime, no guilt.

Learning Along the Way

The leaves were blowing in the wind and catching at the windows as they flew. Rain was lashing down and it had not been light all day. I felt forlorn. There was a fear in my mind and a sadness in my soul. It did not help that the anniversary of the onset of illness for me was in the autumn. I told myself each year that it was a long time ago, and that I had learned how to manage my illness, and that there would never be a replaying of that ghastly time. Yet it was as if my subconscious mind was holding this memory and I was held in fear because of it.

It was now 4.30am and I was sad to see the luminous hands on the clock and acknowledge I was not sleeping well again. I hoped and prayed each year that these frustrating and debilitating symptoms would not develop, but they did! Tired, stressed, oppressed and emotionally vulnerable, the limitedness of this life pulled at my spirit. I hated that this was out of my control. I felt like rolling into a foetal position somewhere safe and warm and dark and not uncurling until the spring.

I had long known that the way to survive and more, the way to wrestle victory from the tragedies and suffering of this world, was to bring them to God and trust what He would do with them. I love the promise that nothing can ever take me away from God, and that He will bring beauty out of ashes (see Isaiah 61:1-3). He will use what we have learned through painful lessons.

I prayed about seasonal affective disorder (SAD), which I suffer from. My GP was encouraging in her acceptance and support of this SAD and recommended a slight change in medication. She recommended a light box, which could be helpful in the mornings. I also received extra prayer support. The condition did not go away, but being supported through it helped me to endure and hold on to hope. As the spring unfurled in the warmth of gentle sunshine, I felt my mood lift. Bubbles of well-being rose in me, and that childlike glow of hope that a season of wonder was coming grew in me.

Our God is a God of surprises, and He can show us aspects of kingdom life that we may not understand.

At an evening meeting at church I was sitting near a lady who was stressed and sad because her husband was terminally ill. Suddenly, as the vicar was speaking, I heard her begin to laugh. She tried to stifle it, but could not. She laughed so much she actually fell out of her chair!

I was intrigued and also impressed at the way the lady's face changed. The stress was gone, her eyes were shining and there was a genuine smile on her face. I wanted to know more. This phenomenon was not something people in church knew about. I had seen it first-hand and I found it appealing. I needed to find out what God's Word said about laughter.

Sarah, the wife of Abraham, after many years of barrenness, was miraculously able to bear a son. She said: 'God has brought me laughter, and everyone who hears about this will laugh with me' (Genesis 21:6). Sarah was acknowledging where her laughter had come from, and how it could be shared.

A verse from Proverbs declares, 'A cheerful heart is good medicine, but a crushed spirit dries up the bones' (Proverbs 17:22). Perhaps the lady I mentioned above received this laughter to strengthen her in her need.

The prophet Nehemiah also said, 'The joy of the LORD is your strength' (Nehemiah 8:10). This reassurance from God gives encouragement, helping us to know that we belong to Him.

I was away on an annual retreat that several young mums went on from our church. Being spared from family commitments gave us a rare opportunity to focus on God. The evening meeting was especially powerful, and I needed to be on my own to respond.

I walked up a hill away from others and saw the sunset. It was so beautiful, yet I responded with tears. I said, 'I don't want to cry, Lord, I want to laugh.' Even as I spoke I felt bubbles of mirth come up from my stomach and burst into my chest. This spontaneous, uncontrolled laughter could not be contained.

I laughed for a long time, my mood lightened, and I felt healed of that deep sadness I had experienced just before. I felt de-stressed, energised and joyful. This laughter had produced inner healing and it also brought me closer to God. I was so grateful to God for this precious gift.

Occasionally this holy laughter returns. I have seen it come at a tense prayer time, where the person being prayed for bursts out laughing, and it spreads to the prayer team. The leader then explains that this is from God and for healing.

Prayer, what a lifeline! I learned the importance of prayer as a baby Christian, when I was first diagnosed with bipolar. There was a real need for protection, healing and provision, which God provided. He also provided people who said, 'We are praying for you.' That was such a powerful phrase for me as I could not pray – my mind would not do it; those faithful people provided my lifeline to God.

Trying to be independent from God would be like turning off the life-support system of an astronaut and expecting him to breathe without oxygen in deep space. We too are a long way from home and we need to keep in good contact with our life support.

I began studying what writers had said about prayer. I was drawn to books which taught about contemplative prayer. This encouraged me on a road I instinctively felt moved towards. It was a struggle to discipline myself to be still and wait upon the Lord, but it was rewarding. I was learning that when you submitted to God and allowed Him to lead you in your prayer times, or any other aspect of your life, you could give control over to Him and He would guide you to bigger truths and not let you down. My vision of God was too small.

As I entered into a time of prayer I began to trust that God would use it. Time with Him was not like time in the world; clocks had no power over Him. I learned to shut the door behind me, to take away distractions and set my will to wait and listen to God.

As I waited I consciously slowed my breathing. Often, distracting thoughts would come. I learned to have a notepad by my side so that I could write those thoughts down and then dismiss them from my mind. I would praise God for His goodness and patience with me and close my eyes and still my spirit again, and wait.

I remember the first time I prayed like this. I was troubled after reading the account of the crucifixion in John 19. I felt hard-hearted. I couldn't take in what had really happened. As Jesus was both human and divine, I felt His experience of the cross would not have been as terrible as it was for those men by His side. It was a real blind moment for me. I pleaded with God to help me understand.

Long silent moments followed as I waited and submitted myself to God. I felt myself being lifted up in my spirit. I was on a cross next to Jesus. My heart raced and I cried out in terror, pleading to be brought down. I felt so ashamed that I had doubted the full enormity of Jesus' suffering. I had been unable to bear a moment on that cross, yet Jesus had suffered for hours in my place. I learned from this that Jesus had taken my place, and I could not take it back. Only He could take that place.

How did I begin to show my love for such a Saviour? Grand one-off gestures would not do. I knew a steady, humble obedience was needed. The prophet Micah said it eloquently: 'He has shown you, O mortal, what is good. And what does the LORD require of you? To act justly and to love mercy and to walk humbly with your God' (Micah 6:8).

I had learned a valuable lesson – if I really wanted to know and understand God, I would need to spend times of retreat away from the noise and distraction of the world on a regular basis, where I would have opportunity to turn my gaze on Him.

There were times when I began to pray about a distressing situation and I would find myself convulsed in tears; my heart felt as if it were breaking. I knew this was not just my imagination, I did not know the area or the people I was praying for, yet my pain was real. It felt like I was part of God's suffering, in fellowship with Him. This is discussed by Joyce Huggett in her book *Listening to God*.[6] We can tune into God's heartbreak that He feels for a needy world. Joyce recommends that we give this pain into the healing hands of Jesus so that His compassion and human heartbreak can meet and be matched.

My experience was that as I groaned and wept it took all my energy, and as I prayed through this time I felt an emptying out of pain and stress. It was clear to me when the prayer was finished. I knew peace then and felt that I had done something God had given me to do. It was as if I was expressing contrition and repentance for the human part of these situations. The Bible tells of a special scroll, which records the tears of the saints, and how highly God values these tears: 'Record my misery; list my tears on your scroll – are they not in your record?' (Psalm 56:8). Malachi tells of a scroll too: 'Then those who feared the LORD talked with each other, and the LORD listened and heard. A scroll of remembrance was written in his presence concerning

---

[6] Joyce Huggett, *Listening to God* (London: Hodder & Stoughton, 1986).

those who feared the LORD and honoured his name' (Malachi 3:16). All is seen and remembered by God.

My longing to pray for others grew as I experienced the desire to see God's kingdom come on earth. I could not bear to see the pain of others without trying to do what I could. My response was to beat on heaven's door. As I listened to God for them and considered His Word, I often received a picture or verse, and a passionate desire to speak out God's will for them.

There were still times when I struggled to retain my equilibrium and I had to say no to some work which I would have liked to have done. I knew the limit of my strength and God had given me discernment to manage my energy and my ability to know what was wise for me to take on. The Lord helped me to stay firm in refusals, when I might have felt pressured to say yes. He told me often, 'It is your love I want more than what you can do for Me.'

I learned that we work not *for* God's favour but *from* His favour. Christians who live out who God tells them they are, cannot be crippled by the opinions of others. They do not need to fit into other people's expectations.

I was away on retreat again, and wondered what the Lord would show me. He surprised me yet again. I was attracted to a workshop on Messianic dance. The rich music and the focus on God really drew me in and I was soon delighted by the experience.

I began a group in church who met to dance each month. Messianic dance was a joy. It was such a powerful thing to submit the physical, mental, emotional and spiritual elements of ourselves to God in worship. Moving in unison with others to worship our God, we brought our will into submission, we felt God's closeness and it was a very special time.

As we learned the steps we laughed at our mistakes and encouraged each other. The laughter and exercise was therapeutic. The worship had a peaceful effect on our hearts and spirits. It seemed very natural at the end of our dancing to kneel and pray.

We noticed that our prayers had a quiet, peaceful sureness about them. It felt like we had entered God's throne room and had His full attention. All barriers had come down as we danced, and our prayers flowed freely – praise changed our perspective of God, and hope rose, no matter how difficult the subject.

Messianic dance was in demand in different clubs. We also held a dance workshop at a church day out, where we danced on the front lawn of a Christian retreat centre, in the splendid grounds of a stately home.

This was the time I began writing more poetry, which helped me to speak out the struggle I lived with. It felt, as I brought these feelings into focus in words, that God was taking away pain; as it came to the surface God was peeling away layers and shining his light into the wounds below. The treatment was cathartic and continues still.

My experience of praying for others was growing, and I became part of the prayer ministry team in my church. I knew the power of prayer, and the need to submit to God. As I listened to him for others he continued to give me words and pictures, feelings and understanding of what He wanted me to tell them about Him and how He felt about them.

People were responding and drawing nearer to God because of prayer. There were times when I felt challenged because I was not healed, but then I was reminded of Paul's teaching to the Church in Corinth: 'My grace is sufficient for you, for my power is made perfect in weakness' (2 Corinthians 12:9). His power was greatest in my weakness and it is through my weakness that I came to a knowledge of my true identity and worth. As I continued to depend upon God, I stayed close to Him and so was more able to allow Him to use me to help others.

I was delighted to attend an evening with Marilyn Baker, the Christian singer-songwriter who is blind. She prayed with me and said God would use me as a channel, but I would need to be brave and confident. I asked God about this. He said: 'You are in this place for a reason; your weakness gives you understanding, hope and faith. You can cope with what I give you, because I am there too; you have the power of heaven at your centre.'

I love the way Jesus can turn our pain into promise, that He can use all that we go through to help others, if we let Him. Pain can diminish who you are, but the prophet Joel writes that the Lord promises: 'I will repay you for the years the locusts have eaten' (Joel 2:25). He gives so much of Himself that pain can be the catalyst through which you can become more like Him. I pondered this and other things God had said to me about healing as I wrote this poem.

Beauty for Ashes

Hallowed ground is the broken heart
Many see it and shy away
Yet Jesus uses such potential treasure
To create the gifting of wounded healers

No easy promise or glib answers will do
Jesus shows us the way in this
Asking that we give what He gives
To be there with the broken

Connecting with hurting hearts and minds
Steadfastly standing with suffering souls
Accepting without judging, you are
Living testimony that life can go on

This is heaven's precious currency,
You must give from a vulnerable place
Learn from your pain, and dare to use
This hard-won compassion, then you will see
Jesus can change your ashes into beauty.

Frightening memories that came from my most dramatic experiences of mania and depression would come back unexpectedly. Now I discovered I could give them to Jesus and they would not return. This was such a freeing prayer, and as I thanked the Lord for His goodness, I had a picture of the church as an outpost of God's kingdom. There was a red cross on the tower. There were soldiers who went out boldly to give the good news of Jesus to any who would receive it. There were also nurses who cared for the wounded. These wounds were spiritual, mental and emotional. The wounds were often old, having been received in childhood. Prayer ministers had the job of leading the wounded to Jesus for healing. The red cross on the church attracted other people, new to the church, who had wounds they knew needed healing. They were welcome and, along with others seeking healing, were introduced to Jesus. Once people were healed, they were able to serve God in the ways he had planned.

This challenged my understanding of how some people may come to faith, and my acceptance of the need to be able to pray with those seeking healing, whether they knew the Lord or not.

I was treating my daughter's skin rash; she had delicate skin and it was difficult to restore the correct balance. I remember feeling passionately that I needed to do something, and I began to pray. I was intent on her healing and I found myself speaking to the infection with authority and commanding it to go. I wept and longed for her skin to be healed, which was the beginning of my seeking the gift of physical healing. Over the years I read and prayed and my longing never left me.

I felt the need to help with family finances. Our daughters were growing and Christmas was coming. My GP said I was unfit for work and supported my application for help. I was not eligible to seek unemployment benefit as I had not done paid work recently. I thought of the work of caring for three children, which was work, but apparently not valued by society!

I applied for the pre-runner of Universal Credit. The assessment forms I filled in focused on physical aspects of health and ability. They also concentrated on measuring the length of time of any disability. By their nature, mental health episodes are more difficult to define, and fluctuate in length and pattern. I felt the questions were loaded against people with mental health issues. I was very disappointed to be told I was not eligible for this either.

I came away from this experience realising that society put no value on me as a person in her own right. I felt devalued, but I knew God and my family and friends did value me. I found part-time work shortly after that and my confidence in being able to commit to paid work grew.

I remember God telling me – as I asked Him at the onset of bipolar, why this was happening – that He was forging a wounded healer. I was not healed of the bipolar, but with medication I managed my condition and lived a useful life – and I knew God's healing in many other areas of my life. I knew the power of prayer and I knew the longing for healing, so a gift of healing continued to be my desire.

Life went on. Our children were growing and I never went back into teaching; my GP advised against it, and I could see the wisdom of this. I did not have the confidence or the stamina to take on a teaching post. So I volunteered at the primary school where our three daughters were being educated. As I helped them on a Monday morning, the children in the class spoke to me about their weekend activities. It became clear that none of the children went to church. This troubled me and I began to pray.

I had hoped that I would begin to feel peace as I prayed, but the opposite happened. I began to grieve and I wrestled in my prayer times. One day I cried out to God for Him to do something, and He spoke into my anguish, 'You do something!' I was shocked. Dare I ignore that command? I considered it and decided I could not. I asked the Lord to show me what I had to do. And that is when I saw God at work in so many ways, guiding, leading and connecting other people in to the same vision.

This was an exciting adventure. It took hold of my heart and taught me how God can take ordinary people and lead them into unexpected places. God guided me into meetings with people I was rather intimidated by, and I came out of these meetings with their support.

There were 'God incidences' and provision, and my excitement grew along with my expectation. The vision enlarged as people stepped forward to become part of the plan. With much prayer support, we began a Quest Club in my local primary school. This was a voluntary club held at lunchtime for any child who wanted to find out about Jesus.

Our team saw faith grow in a hungry land; so many children came who knew nothing of Jesus. They came on a quest and many found treasure. It was a huge privilege to share our love of Jesus and to see their response to Him.

I remember one child who came running across the playground at the start of a meeting. He could barely control his excitement as he told me of an answer to the prayer he had prayed at a difficult family moment the night before. He was convinced that Jesus had answered his prayer.

There were challenges and some persecution along the way, but many children came and faithfully stayed with us for years.

The staff in the school were also impacted and we saw amazing changes in their response to us. Initially some were unfriendly, suspicious and resentful of the children who chose to come, but over the years of prayer and witness and faithfulness to the children, their response changed to acceptance, helpfulness and trust.

We were given display boards around the school, and we led assemblies with the children, which were full of God's love. One day we sang a Spirit-filled song, feeling very daring, and to our delight the head teacher asked us to teach it to the school. So we sang it repeatedly and left the music with them. We finished our clubs – there were two in the end – eight years later as the school was included in a county-wide schools Christian initiative.

During this adventure, my faith had been stretched beyond any previous experience. I had learned how to step out in faith, to pray for miracles and to see them happen. But gradually I could detect a change in the way I responded to the work. I felt as if the anointing, which had given me confidence, was no longer there. At the same time I was being pulled in another direction.

I began to experience tingling in my hands as I raised them in worship. The sensitivity grew to the point of discomfort. I checked this strange experience with a Christian doctor who laughed and asked if the tingling happened at other times. 'No,' I told her, 'only when worshipping in church.' She reassured me that there was nothing medically wrong.

This sensitivity had the effect of raising my awareness of God's desire to heal. When I prayed with people for physical healing, a new sensation grew; when I prayed and laid hands on them, there was a great compulsion to touch the place of pain, however gently. As I gained permission to do this, I could feel changes happening in that area, and often my hands would grow hot or cold; this would be passed on to the person being healed.

People began to say that pain had gone, or that there was an improvement in their condition; others would give testimony later that God had healed them. It gave me great joy to see others receive God's healing. I was deeply humbled to think that God wanted to use me in my incomplete healing.

The prophet Malachi speaks of healing for those who revere the Lord's name on the Day of the Lord: 'But for you who revere my name, the sun of righteousness will rise with healing in its rays. And you will go out and frolic like well-fed calves' (Malachi 4:2). As a child I had lived on a farm and near a calves' enclosure, and I remember being much impressed as I watched them being released. They seemed to change into other creatures as they jumped and bucked and bounded for joy, suddenly invigorated with the thrill of being free. I smile whenever I read that verse, and I know I will be free of my illness one day. The Bible tells us there is no mental or physical illness in heaven (see Revelation 21:4).

Our pastoral team in church went on a weekend retreat to listen and pray, and it was during this time that a picture was given to me. This picture showed myself as a phoenix rising from the ashes. It spoke to my spirit and I was moved to write this poem inspired from illness, but going on to very different experiences.

Phoenix

The restraints were gone, I flew too high
Spent I fell, helpless
Mind and soul were out of control
Defenceless I plummeted to earth
Breathless, shattered, lifeless.

Fire all around, pain beyond believing
Silence for a long time, nothing left but ashes.

Was I breathing?
Slowly I began to feel, a mass of hurting
Too many wounds to count, hard and sore
I lay empty, waiting.

God breathed into me
Time began to turn again for me
Life began anew.

I wanted to make this new life count
To receive new gifts
And gain new understanding.

My passion was healing,
I knew God had healed me
I knew His heart for the hurting
I began to weep for the wounded
To believe for the hopeless
And lay hands on the sick

Tingling in my hands began
I asked doctors if this could be explained

When I worship my hands come alive
I am convicted to touch the hurting area
I feel God's power at work and I am humbled
As I share the joy of a person's healing.

My vicar asked me to be a church visitor for someone who was in hospital suffering a psychological episode. I wondered how it would feel to be faced with this, my first visit to someone with a mental health issue. I recognised some of the symptoms – paranoia, delusions, hallucinating – and as he talked I was able to empathise and reassure. I was able to spend a number of hours listening to him and I knew he found this helpful. I found this time rewarding and fulfilling. He recovered from this episode and continued with his life, and I realised I had a part to play in supporting those with mental health issues.

I had been caring for someone who suffered deeply from depression, and this caring had deepened my empathy. I had met and prayed with a lady who suffered from bipolar in a distant city; now I was asked to pray with someone in our church who suffered from bipolar, who I would be able to see regularly – and she was my age. It had taken years, but finally one of my longings was realised. I now knew a Christian who suffered bipolar who I could share with deeply, and it was so good.

I was more confident in managing my own health, and from my experience of helping others, I now felt able to seek God for what He wanted me to do. I began to form a vision for mental health support in churches. I remembered the isolation I felt when I was newly diagnosed, and the positive experiences of later meeting other Christian bipolar sufferers, and knew this was part of what God wanted me to be involved in.

God's timing in our lives is of fundamental importance; the longings of years were becoming crystallised in my thinking and in my spirit. People were coming to me in growing numbers to ask for prayer regarding mental health, and my awareness of their needs grew.

At the same time our pastoral leader in church brought three of us together who had approached her about mental health issues. We three began to pray. We met often and the vision grew.

God has a special place in His heart for those who struggle with their mental health, so there should be a special place among His people for them to meet to be supported; a place from which to challenge God's people about ignorance, prejudice and fear, and to bring something positive out of suffering.

We gave out a questionnaire asking people for feedback about mental health support in church, and the response showed us there was a need for a meeting place where people could be heard. Mental health issues can be frightening and deeply isolating and those who suffer may have to face stigma, or feel abandoned to their fate, by those who could help them if only they were encouraged and trained in how to do this.

I had heard too many times of others who had been made to feel ashamed of their mental vulnerability, who had succumbed to the stigma surrounding mental ill health. Stigma was a big problem for many sufferers, and it was clear that we would need to challenge this in our church. Jesus challenged Nicodemus because he was ignorant about being born of the Spirit, and He taught him valuable lessons so he could then teach others (see John 3).

Prejudice was another issue Jesus dealt with, and He was always telling people not to fear. So the ignorance, prejudice and fear that work together to cause the ugly effects of stigma had to be challenged.

Solomon wrote: 'For he will deliver the needy who cry out, the afflicted who have no one to help ... He will rescue them from oppression and violence, for precious is their blood in his sight' (Psalm 72:12,14). God does not condemn Christians because they have depression, so neither can we. Let us guard against being a hindrance, and choose how we can be of help.

As the three of us met and prayed and the vision grew, we were sometimes overwhelmed at the challenge we were taking on. We felt we might be inadequate, and we listened deeply to God's guidance. Colin Urquhart, in his book *The Positive Kingdom*, spoke of the cost being in giving before you know what will happen. This is essential in kingdom life. To share what we have with others. And it is faith to trust that this will be good.[7] It was costly to lay down our fears and to step out in faith not knowing where our journey would lead us, but we were travelling hopefully.

One night as we were praying, a direct command to 'stand up' was whispered quite fiercely in my ear by an unseen presence, so that is what we did. Later we read a verse in Joshua: 'The LORD said to Joshua, "Stand up! what

---

[7] Colin Urquhart, *The Positive Kingdom* (London: Hodder & Stoughton, 1985).

are you doing down on your face?"' (Joshua 7:10). This gave us the confidence to know we were doing God's will and this was God's timing. Now was the time to be bold.

OK to Be Me

I can dream big dreams and I believe God gives these dreams to me, but I can also get very tired. I try to manage my life in the full knowledge that I have a diagnosis of bipolar. Sometimes I get my priorities mixed and the need to be the best that I can be for the Lord can lead me to lose sight of my particular safe limits. I need to say no to those who would make me overcommitted in their own vision, and do so without guilt. I need to be clear in my priorities.

Now that we three leaders had come to a point of starting our mental health support in church, obtrusive thoughts came to trouble and challenge us: 'Who do you think you are? What can you do? You are ill and weak and useless. You have no idea how difficult this will be, you could be out of your depth, and you could do harm.'

We went to the Lord with all of this attack from the enemy. He reminded us that we have known this foreign land called mental illness. He had brought us through it with insight and understanding of what it is to suffer mental ill health. We had empathy and we were all prayer ministers, and we were able to bring those suffering to Him for healing.

God told us to look beyond the diagnosis and love the person underneath. Where there is love there is no fear. He also gave us the verse: 'Have I not commanded you? Be strong and courageous. Do not be afraid; do not be discouraged, for the LORD your God will be with you wherever you go' (Joshua 1:9). We might have been the strangest-looking warriors, but we held on to that promise that God would be with us and aimed to keep Him central in all that we did.

The challenges of beginning this support group came mostly from inside us. When I felt inadequate I asked the Lord to build my self-worth. He said, 'I am in you, and you are in Me, therefore I give you My worth.' We were conscious of needing God in all that we were beginning to do. You have to be prepared to sacrifice what you are in order to become what God wants you to be. Something inside you says 'I will' even when those around you say 'you can't'. Start where you are and with what you have, then God will give you more. If you wait to have enough before you move, you may wait forever.

We analysed the questionnaire we had sent out in church to ask people if they would like a support group for those who suffered with mental health issues. The response was positive, so we finalised the plans and, with the agreement of leadership, set a date for our first meeting.

We set about defining just what we believed God was asking us to do and these aims became our guiding principles.

The aims of the Mental Health Fellowship were to provide:

- A place of welcome and belonging
- An atmosphere of acceptance and respect
- A place of understanding and encouragement
- An atmosphere of compassion
- Opportunity for mutual support and sharing
- A chance to enjoy and celebrate together
- Information about mental health issues and services
- A chance to give as well as receive
- Opportunity to develop the Christian journey of faith
- Space for prayer

We spoke at each service in church on the Sunday before the inaugural meeting.

We designed information cards, which were displayed in the church foyer to inform new people about the group, and delivered posters by hand to other churches, introducing ourselves. We also contacted doctors' surgeries and the local hospital, particularly the psychiatric unit.

The Mental Health Fellowship began on 9th November 2004. It was held in St Thomas Church in Kendal. Our first meeting had nine members, some from our own church, but others from surrounding churches and some who professed no spiritual faith. I still remember the thankfulness I felt that people would trust us and come to the group, and that God would use this space to do His kingdom work. People were generous in sharing and eager to give from a vulnerable place. This first meeting was richly blessed and we rejoiced that we had begun.

We could talk easily about illness; this was the one place members felt they could talk openly and freely and still rely on an empathetic response. In the group they could lower all protective barriers.

The group designed a logo that featured on all our literature. It stated boldly 'OK TO BE ME'. We aimed to affirm all people in this, giving them permission to be who God had made them to be.

We described the group in our publicity as 'A self-help support group for those with mental health difficulties and their carers'. We developed our programme of activities which included talks and visiting speakers, teaching CDs, creative days for members' interests, talks and demonstrations, walks and visiting local places of interest. We were able to do this through grants from local charities, whose representatives recognised the value of the group and wanted to support us.

We encouraged the members to take an active part in all areas of the group. We asked the members what they would like to study and learn when planning each programme. Volunteers were encouraged to lead on any subject that interested them. We found personal testimony and experience of illness were powerful ways of informing others; it challenged all of us to be better informed and more tolerant.

The church supported us in free accommodation and refreshments. It was important to offer free access to the group, as a number of members were living on benefits and were unable to work because of their issues.

The need to inform those in our congregations who did not have experience of caring for someone with mental health needs or problems themselves was very evident. We heard from those who came to the group of how they had been treated with suspicion by some in their churches, as though they were infectious. They were very aware of stigma, which was a barrier between them and some of their fellow Christians. We came to see that fear and ignorance had to be challenged in such a way that these barriers would be broken down. We looked at how Jesus had put an end to fear, prejudice and ignorance by getting alongside people, by accepting and loving them and showing them a better way.

Our meetings included testimonies from anyone who felt able to share them. Knowing that credibility must precede gaining the group's trust and the ability to communicate freely, I knew I had to speak first. As I stepped out in faith, making myself vulnerable, I saw people responding empathically through their facial expressions and by the quality of their listening. As I had become vulnerable in my sharing I was rewarded with other people beginning to share and engage with the group.

We decided our guidelines for the group the first day. We kept it short: only three rules, and we displayed them as an aide-memoire every week. The rules were part of our ethos of caring, respecting each other, valuing each other, being prepared to share and maintaining confidentiality within the group.

Guidelines for the group:

- Treat everyone with dignity and honour
- Respect the views of others (even if you do not agree with them)
- Confidentiality must be kept within the group

As leaders, we set up boundaries for the group. We stated that we would be available each Monday between 1pm and 2.30pm in the church lounge. The group would have a Christian ethos; non-Christians were welcome if they could respect our beliefs. We felt it was important to set clear boundaries regarding our availability to members of the group outside of the meeting time. Some members were not good at keeping their own personal boundaries and in their vulnerability had great need, which we could not meet, nor would it have been good for them if we did.

Occasionally members were hospitalised, and we decided it was important to visit them in order to extend care when they were feeling extremely vulnerable. We agreed to keep this care consistent for all members. We also encouraged the members to visit each other in hospital.

Some members felt isolated and we encouraged them to meet outside of group meetings. One common cause of concern was visiting their GP. When they needed to visit their doctor they began to feel anxious, so we discussed this in the group. If they were feeling in a low mood or particularly fearful, then they felt daunted by trying to describe how they felt.

Several members said they wrote down key words or a list for discussion. This helped them to feel more prepared and less anxious, and helped them not to forget important points to talk about with the doctor. We looked at descriptive words that might help members of the group to be open and honest about how they were feeling. We also encouraged people to put a timeline together for when significant changes had happened in their lives. All these would be helpful for their GP to know. Practicalities, such as the length of journey to the surgery, needed to be considered. Members would need to allow sufficient time so that they were not rushing, and did not feel anxious before they met the GP. We asked people to consider if they wanted to take a friend or relative with them, and talked about who they might ask. Occasionally, leaders of our group or other members would accompany them.

The long-term members with chronic illness would sometimes want to have more contact than a weekly meeting. They were instructed that in an emergency they could contact the church office who would pass on the request. In that way we could decide about the suitability of contacting these members and when it was possible for us to do so. This was respected, and I found that a timely word and listening when a member was distressed could build confidence and reduce their feelings of isolation, and help them manage that crisis time. We did not offer home visits or practical help in the home as we felt this would be beyond our resources. There was another group in church who would offer visits and practical help.

Confidentiality was most important. All members were expected to keep everything that was discussed in the group, 'in the group'. I also kept the knowledge of attendance and medical details confidential, and contact details for members were stored securely. This was not to make the group secret, but to ensure people knew that their views and experiences would be confined within the group, fostering an expectation that it was safe to share in the group and that this would be honoured.

As we got to know the members, we found many to be capable of courage and greatness of spirit; their faith was strong enough to endure through times of great suffering, and their acceptance and love of God in the midst of this could teach all of us an important lesson.

Dependence on God means that without God's grace we cannot live an abundant life. Many in the group knew that; their faith had been tested repeatedly through episodes of illness where they experienced deep suffering, yet they still continued to walk humbly with God. I and the other leaders were honoured to listen and to pray with them.

The prayer time for the group was held towards the end of the meeting, deliberately, to allow those who did not want to participate to leave more easily and without pressure. When we prayed with members we split into small groups, trying to be sensitive as to who might pray well together. We shared the needs for prayer, and everyone who felt called to pray did so. The compassion shown as members prayed for each other, some with stumbling words, sighs and pauses, was all part of God's healing process.

If there were further needs for prayer, two leaders, both trained prayer ministers, would be available. This would be after the meeting or at another time during the week at a mutually convenient time. We needed to listen carefully and ask what the person wanted prayer for. It would have been presumptuous and unhelpful to assume we knew. The Lord would often show us the underlying problem. We would pray against the specific causes of their illness by praying for the opposite to come. In depression, people often look at their lives with distorted lenses. We would gently challenge this, offering what the Lord was telling us about their lives. Where there was distortion, we would pray for a new perspective, and an improved clarity of vision for them.

Because depression was often seen as a weakness or personality failing, we would always seek to build people up with God's affirming words. We would finish with a blessing on their relationships with God, themselves and others.

We knew we needed to keep the prayer time short and clear, as the person being prayed for may have had poor concentration and low levels of energy if they were struggling with depression. It was wonderful to see when those members who were prayed with showed signs of improvement and healing.

One problem that occurred for some members of the Mental Health Fellowship was the issue of stopping medication. This was usually without medical supervision. The sudden withdrawal of antidepressants or other drugs led to the person feeling very afraid and their experiencing mood swings. This could lead to dangerous activities and self-harm. We encouraged them to go back to their GP. On some occasions I would go with them if they requested it. They would be reassured by their doctor and set on another course of medication. This medication might take a month to take effect, and so they would be particularly vulnerable during this period. At these times we would encourage other members of the group to partner with those who were struggling, to see them socially and to encourage them to go for walks. They were offered appointments to come into church for listening and prayer, and signposted to other mental health charities in the community.

When one of our members did feel particularly ill we would plan our activities to help them. Our aim was to support them, but also to be clear in our boundaries so that expectations were clearly established on both sides. We could not fix the person, but we would try to help them in their journey of recovery and to well-being.

Helplessness was a feeling, not a fact. So we challenged that by encouraging the person to work at their own pace towards goals that they set themselves. Catastrophising was something else we had to challenge. We encouraged the person to acknowledge that there were some good things in their situation; not all was bad.

We also discussed in the group how you could move from simple directed chores to taking more responsibility. Someone who had experienced depression would lack confidence, so the group would bring their experience of this problem and we pooled our wisdom and knowledge.

One example we discussed was how someone could go from going out to a local shop to buy one item to eventually spending more time in a supermarket. These were tasks that many would be able to achieve without much conscious thought, but for others they were major expeditions. We looked at developing concentration, improving communications and using time well.

Prayer was an important aspect of health and we shared in the group how someone might go from not being able to pray, which was a common experience when members were unwell, to praying for others.

Accepting prayer from others was the first step; submitting to the care of others and trusting them to speak to God for them. Taking some responsibility and asking for prayer was another important step. The next was to pray for their own needs independently. The final stage was taking that big step of looking outside of their own needs and praying for others.

Group activities at such times were usually creative, as working with their hands would often encourage people to share without being self-conscious.

We found that writing and talking was the best way to undermine the stigma surrounding mental health issues, as only by sharing our experiences could we help others to understand and accept and not be afraid of the idea of mental illness. We wanted to help people in the church to see stigma as an important social, medical and spiritual challenge that needed to be addressed.

As we grew together as a group, we held a workshop where we looked at how we could raise awareness of mental health needs in the church; we also considered how we could increase our involvement in its life. I had devised these questions for a study day that had recently been held in our area where representatives from churches had taken part. I was eager to see how our group would respond to them. Working in groups we looked at several questions:

1. In what ways can those with enduring mental health issues be brought into the life of the church?

It was decided that the church leadership needed to be actively involved in promoting a positive ethos, by stating that they supported people with mental health issues in the church's mission statement, and outlining how they would do this.

One suggestion was that a quiet corner be made available after church services for those who did not feel comfortable in a busy refreshments queue. A helpful initiative would be if a volunteer could be available to answer any questions about the sermon or talk.

It was thought that services during the year with a mental health focus, including biblical examples of mental distress, would be helpful. This could include teaching on supporting those with mental health needs.

We noted that the best way of encouraging people with mental health issues into church was to greet them, befriend them, and invite them to all activities where there would be provision for specific needs. The group decided to be as proactive as possible in teams such as 'Messy Church' and seasonal activities, for example, the Christmas choir. I discussed with the leaders of these projects how our members could be included and encouraged in these activities.

2. How well does your church care for people with depression and anxiety? What more could be done?

The group were happy that the Mental Health Fellowship provided specific support and that the church supported us by giving us free accommodation.

The group was helped by the pastoral leader of the church, who supervised me in my leadership role, and by other leaders in the group, which gave the group its strong foundation.

We considered how to advertise the group. PowerPoint slides displayed in church before and after services would be one way. Writing articles for the church magazine was also a possibility. Placing printed cards in the foyer of the church for newcomers to take away with them was another good way of informing people about the group and its activities.

We also felt that the NHS Community Mental Health Team could be encouraged to visit the group and speak to the wider church membership. This we did and invited church leaders and other interested people to join us. This had the added advantage of promoting the group to health professionals.

3. To what degree do people have to be 'fixed' to be able to serve in the church family?

It was suggested that no one is ever perfectly ready to serve. Everyone needs to be allowed to say when they feel ready. Care would need to be taken to fit people in to service where they were most comfortable.

Once a member of the group was established in their place of service, they would need a supporter to work in the same area. The safeguarding officer in the church could oversee anyone serving in this way. Regular supervision meetings would encourage feedback, both from the church and the person. Support in this way would be very useful, and the person could tell the supervisor if they needed a break.

4. To what extent might sin influence depression and anxiety, and how can we deal with this?

Some members of the group were rather offended by this question. So we broke it down and accepted that anyone who sins is distanced from God, whether they are suffering from depression or not. One symptom of depression can be that you feel isolated from God and from everyone, so this makes it more difficult to know if it is sin that may be causing this feeling of isolation, or the depression.

We decided the best way of dealing with this feeling was to use God's remedy for sin. When we confess and repent of sin, God promises to forgive us. The difficulty lies in believing that truth when our feelings do not change, and we do not experience God's forgiveness.

To help us in this we agreed to seek to have a close relationship with God, and when we were aware of sin, to bring it to Him in prayer. We also agreed to be accountable to each other. We gathered affirming Bible verses and kept them readily available in meetings. Some people placed them on their mirrors at home, so they could be encouraged every day.

5. What would be the strengths and weaknesses of specific fellowship groups in churches for those with depression and anxiety?

We decided that if a separate group was not outward-looking, it could be isolated and there would be few opportunities where stigma, prejudice and ignorance could be challenged. This helped us to be more determined to raise the profile of the group by serving in the life of the church.

The strengths of a separate group, we decided, were that you could share deeply about the difficulties of living with mental distress and know that you were being heard by people who shared some of these difficulties.

Empathy was acknowledged as very important. This helped build a feeling of identity and acceptance. It helped build relationships within the group. This encouraged close fellowship for those who struggled with feelings of belonging.

Confidentiality within the group helped people to feel safe, and helped promote a willingness to be vulnerable and real with each other. This too helped relationships to grow.

Within a separate group, members could choose what subjects to study, and what specialist information, books and signposting to community mental health services and mental health charities were available. This would not be possible with a more general group within the church.

Walking groups or other activity-based groups in the church would offer social interaction which was valuable, but may not have been suited to our members' capabilities.

We resolved to go on walks and do other physical activities within the group.

This workshop had been most valuable, and we endeavoured to put into action the suggestions that were made.

An Ongoing Adventure

We occasionally performed drama in the group. We wrote scripts and improvised sketches. It helped to express the problems we encountered in our own lives, and work through the answers to problems.

Humour was very effective here, as we could tackle common problems and make fun of people's misconceptions. The cause of depression was one aspect we looked at. We acknowledged that when there was no attributable cause, it would frustrate other people who seemed to need there to be one.

We acted out the frustrations of receiving advice which had not been sought, and when given, was inappropriate, ineffective and showed a lack of understanding of the nature of depression. 'Putting a brave face on it' and 'counting your blessings' were two such examples.

It was amazing how quickly a sketch could move from pathos to humour. It was valuable to be able to work through these conflicting emotions. It was affirming to be able to speak out at injustice and the ignorance of those who did not know what it was like to live with mental distress.

One such sketch was gifted to us to use by Rob who created drama for our church. *Them Dolphins* explored issues of mental health. This short extract from the sketch gives examples of the misunderstandings that exist around mental illness.

> Two friends are talking, one has just come back from holiday.
> **One** is confiding to the other that he is feeling depressed.
> **Two** is trying to discover the cause of his friend's low mood.

> **One**: No, that's the problem. Everything is going fine, but I just feel really low.
> **Two**: You should go for a run.
> **One**: A run?
> **Two**: Yeh, go for a run – it will make you feel better. Exercise apparently releases them dolphins or something.
> **One**: I think you mean endorphins. They're a substance released in your brain at certain times that make you feel better.
> **Two**: That's it. I thought that it sounded a bit strange, but dolphins always seem happy, don't they, so if they were released you would feel better?
> **One**: Hmmm.
> **Two**: Why don't you talk to someone about it?
> **One**: Stress, depression, mental illness – they all have a stigma attached to them.
> **Two**: Oh they're painful, them stigmas. My friend had one. He had to go to the doctors to have it cut off!

One: If I talked to someone about it, it would be a sign of weakness.

Two: I know what you should do, you should pray about it. Perhaps you have got some unconfessed sin in there.

One: How long can I keep on pretending to be OK? Oh God, please help me! Will someone just help?[8]

The above sketch promoted many useful discussions within the congregation after being performed in a service.

We worked under the acceptance, encouragement and provision of the pastoral leader and the leadership of the church. I had supervision meetings with the pastoral leader and a GP, so when difficult issues arose I could discuss these and receive guidance from them. This was very important, as I needed to be accountable in my leadership of the group in a confidential setting.

Being able to be accountable like this and have decisions I had made affirmed was very encouraging and built my confidence. It also enabled any wrong actions to be checked and put right quickly. The pastoral leader as a managerial supervisor was able to keep me informed of issues in the wider church and helped us to keep in step with other departments, and link up with other work that could be of help to our group.

I attended weekly staff meetings at church, as this was a useful information-sharing meeting. This also enabled me to keep up to date with the bigger church picture, which I could share with the group, encouraging them to

---

[8] Written by Robert Funning, and quoted with his permission.

feel part of what was going on. This meeting also gave me the opportunity to talk with all members of staff, with whom I developed excellent links, and encourage them to have input into the group. This fostered an acceptance of the Mental Health Fellowship among church staff and an understanding of the work we were doing.

As our presence in the church grew, we found opportunities to talk with many people individually. We took our place on the church after-service coffee rota as we had agreed to do in a previous workshop. Some members read selected Bible passages at the front of church, and we also obtained permission to lead some services. These services were based on aspects of mental health, where members of the group would take part.

This was helpful in gaining the attention of all the church and we found many people would come to talk to us about their own experiences and were able to gain information and support.

It also helped those brave members of our group who had stood up and boldly witnessed to the congregation to feel empowered, and that they had something of value to give to others, and so received something for themselves that was affirming and positive.

We were invited to contribute to the church magazine, so we described what we did in the group and the varied activities available. We also asked members to say why they came. This was a useful way of addressing the areas of prejudice, ignorance and fear that existed even in the church family.

Our teaching in church services included defining mental health. The Church of England Archbishops'

Council in 2004 defined mental health as 'Emotional and spiritual resilience, which enables us to enjoy life and survive pain, disappointment and sadness. It is a positive sense of wellbeing and underlying belief in our own worth and the dignity and worth of others.'[9] This was a more holistic definition than many clinical ones and a very positive statement, involving aspects of character that were not usually used or seen as important in mental health definitions.

We would use visual ways to explain that physical illness and disability are easy to see, to try to understand and to help, but that when the mind is ill it is harder to see the wound or know how to help.

We then talked about the mental health spectrum and that we were all on it. We could move away from mental well-being because of new situations that cause stress and lowering of mood. Situations change and so does our mental health. No one can take mental health for granted. Paul said, 'Carry each other's burdens, and in this way you will fulfil the law of Christ' (Galatians 6:2). We encouraged questions and comments from the congregation. Testimony from members of the group and their own prayers were an important part of the message.

One attitude we knew must be addressed was that some Christians believed mental illness to be a response by a vengeful God on sinful behaviour. Sin separated us from God, it was true, but repentance led to forgiveness and

---

[9] 'The Church of England Archbishops Council Report', 2004. Definition of mental health. www.cofe.anglican.org/info/social public/home affairs/mental health/parish resource (accessed 29th November 2017).

restoration. Mental illness was no more a result of one person's specific sin than cancer may be to that person. (See also John 9, the story of the man born blind, that I mentioned earlier.) We all fall short of God's standards (see Romans 3:23), and because of this, He sent Jesus to rescue, atone for and restore our relationship with Himself.

This condemning attitude some people show towards mental health issues can be harmful to people suffering from depression, because a symptom of depression can be that you feel separated from everything. Your low mood will make it likely that you will believe the person who tells you it is your own fault that you are depressed, and God is punishing you. This is when you need the Holy Spirit to convict you that you are chosen, accepted and loved, and for others to come alongside, accepting and loving you just as you are. It is the role of a loving church family.

One characteristic of mental distress is fear. It is present in many different illnesses. The fear caused by hearing negative voices, or of persistent isolation, or the dread of being mentally out of control can be disempowering. We looked at fear from a biblical perspective and noted that in its positive sense, it is actually a useful gift from God – it can keep us from doing things that would be harmful to us; the 'flight or fight' response. The group then defined fear as an unpleasant emotion caused by the threat of danger, pain or harm. We also noted that our enemy, Satan, liked to keep us bound in fear. But Jesus often told people He met not to fear, but to have faith.

The psalmist encouraged us. 'God is our refuge and strength, an ever-present help in trouble. Therefore we will not fear, though the earth give way and the mountains fall into the heart of the sea' (Psalm 46:1-2). What empowering verses, which called us to come close to God and trust Him whatever the circumstances!

We looked at the story of Jesus as He went to the cross. Jesus was determined and focused, yet in Gethsemane He showed His fear of what lay ahead. He rose above His fear to fulfil His destiny. We also discussed what the story of Peter told us about fear. Peter had a terrible time when Jesus was arrested. He wanted to be courageous but fear had the upper hand. He denied that he knew Jesus. Yet Peter got a second chance. Jesus forgave and commissioned Peter who became the leader of His Church (see John 18 and 21). This encouraged the group, believing Jesus would forgive us when we confessed our fears to Him and lead us to better health and well-being.

The prophet Isaiah tells us that God said, '[I will] bestow on them … a garment of praise instead of a spirit of despair' (Isaiah 61:3). We felt called to worship, which drew us closer to God, so that fear went and we were strengthened in our faith. It was reassuring that God understood our fear and that we could bring our weaknesses to Him.

John tells us 'perfect love drives out fear' (1 John 4:18). Trust and faith in Jesus is very important. The group agreed that if we stayed close to Jesus we would be less likely to feel fear. This led to a prayer time where we confessed our fears and asked Jesus to replace the fears with His perfect love.

The Bible illustrates that God does not distance Himself from depressed people. Job was honest in his feelings during great personal tragedy and suffered depression;

King David suffered highs and lows and expressed them beautifully in the Psalms; also Solomon and Elijah testify to this. Elijah, in the aftermath of a great victory over the prophets of Baal, went and hid in the desert, exhausted and afraid, and asked God to end his life. God answered his plea by sending an angel carer, who fed, comforted and encouraged Elijah, until he was healed and restored (see 1 Kings 19:1-9).

We saw earlier that Solomon wrote: 'For he will deliver the needy who cry out, the afflicted who have no one to help. He will take pity on the weak and the needy and save the needy from death. He will rescue them from oppression and violence, for precious is their blood in his sight' (Psalm 72:12-14). God does not condemn Christians because they have depression, so neither can we. Let us be wary of being a hindrance to healing, and decide how we might help one another.

We set up a support team for the group; our prayer coordinator assigned intercessors for general and more specific prayer, and the church ladies' group took up the challenge too. As the group was confidential, identities were not disclosed without permission. This helped us to know, along with our own prayers, that we were being supported. The work was challenging and sudden problems could arise, but it was strengthening to know God was in charge.

We were invited to attend the Mental Health Forum for Statutory and Voluntary services in our local area. This gave me an opportunity to meet representatives from key agencies. The first time I went to the forum I found the language used a barrier, but with persistence it became less so. Our commitment as volunteers was appreciated. I found the opportunity to talk to individuals from agencies very helpful; to have a person with whom I could make contact encouraged communication. Being accepted as you are as someone with something worth saying was as affirming at these meetings as it must have been for the Mental Health Fellowship members at our meetings.

From these gatherings we were able to draw speakers for the group, along with up-to-date information and awareness of other local mental health initiatives. Most importantly, though, were the personal contacts and links which led to an acceptance of our group in the community. We began to get referrals from GPs, community psychiatric nurses and leaders of other voluntary mental health groups and housing associations. We wrote articles for the forum's magazine and our contact details were included in their directory.

I was invited to attend the Cumbria Mental Health group meetings for service users and carers. This enabled me to represent the needs of our group to a body that reported to local government. It also enabled us to keep up to date with issues of changing funding, benefits and services. I encouraged our group members to attend, to be involved with these important issues and to feel empowered and have their say.

I had opportunity to complete a Community Mental Health Care course, which was helpful and enabled me to meet and work with social workers, CPNs, psychiatric nurses, and voluntary sector workers in the area. I was encouraged to find they treated me as an equal, even though I did not have their qualifications. They found my experiences with the Fellowship interesting and welcomed my inclusion in the group.

The Mental Health Fellowship welcomed sixty people from churches and secular organisations, overall. Some attended the fellowship for a short time, recovered, and were able to resume work and a normal life. Often people stayed with us for years. We met many people with long-term mental health issues. The full spectrum of mental illness was represented in the group. I remember what the Lord said to us about seeing past the illness to the person behind. People with the same diagnosis may have the same symptoms, but will react to them differently, and have different experiences of faith. All are unique, and it is not until you know the person better that you can help them.

Imagine in your church on Sunday morning the following scenario. A person standing alone in the corner is known to be schizophrenic; people are avoiding him as he stares at them and is muttering to himself. He is anxious, as he does not like crowds. But there is another perspective to this person.

His name is Paul and he has some endearing qualities. He suffers quietly; he would not hurt anyone. Paul has the courage to go on; he believes God is in every part of his life, even through terrible times. He needs our love, respect and support. He also has a story from which we can learn, and he has a lot to give. He has a diagnosis of schizophrenia, but this does not define all that he is. Jesus knows this. Do we?

We always felt that the Mental Health Fellowship was a very special place and were protective of the group. I knew that I needed to monitor the people who came, as the wrong person could damage the precious healing work that went on there. I would meet with a new referral to see if the group would be helpful to them and if they would manage to fit in. I would collect some confidential information about their mental health history and a contact person for them. This might be their GP or CPN and I explained that we would become part of their care support. With their agreement, I would contact their other support workers if we were concerned about a worsening of their condition. It was a helpful time for each of us, as the interviewee could assess whether they were going to benefit from the group. Only very rarely would a person be denied access, due to extreme ill health, which made it difficult for them to cooperate within a group situation, or known convictions of the person, which may have become a safety issue for the group.

We had many adventures, challenging one another and accepting one another, and we all learned along the way. We learned about one another and we learned about ourselves. Apart from the experience of mental ill health, the thing many of us had in common was faith in God, even though that was expressed in different ways. '"Because he loves me," says the LORD, "I will rescue him; I will protect him, for he acknowledges my name. He will call on me, and I will answer him; I will be with him in trouble' (Psalm 91:14-15). I used this in my testimony and others in this group identified with it too; it can be true for anyone who trusts and depends on God.

God was telling us that we could depend on Him to protect us and He would never let us down. He would be with us in our episodes of illness and not leave us. The requirement was that we were faithful in return. We must speak to others about Him, and do our part in maintaining a relationship with Him.

A favourite verse was 'I will give you treasures of darkness, riches stored up in secret places, so that you may know that I am the LORD, the God of Israel, who summons you by name' (Isaiah 45:3, NIV 1984). The group found it difficult to enter into contemplative prayer together, but when we attempted this it was valuable to some people. We all acknowledged our fragility and weakness in our illness, but that only caused us to rely on God more.

As we shared what God had spoken to us during prayer, we were deeply grateful. This is what He told us: 'If you want to find out how strong God's arm is, you need to lean all your weight on it.' This was very reassuring for those who felt so weak during episodes of ill health. This was affirming and faith-building for us.

When you knew you had nothing to give to God in your illness, He protected, restored and healed you. Why? Because you were His and He loved you.

God did important work in our difficult times; like seeds grown in the dark, we found new gifts developing in us. We found that empathy could usually be expressed most effectively by those who knew the pain of suffering. We learned that dependence and humility were hard-won but prized spiritual qualities.

The times when we were unable to communicate with others in illness gave us greater need to reach out to God. The Lord in His great mercy showed us that however the world thought of people with mental health issues, He saw us as we were, and knew us by our names. God dignified us in our suffering, by sharing our pain, and His presence enabled our faith to grow. Our faith felt central to us and we could draw on it as we felt the need. It seemed that our faith could not be shaken because it was the result of having been shaken. We could look for treasure every day, and if we looked as God sees, we could receive encouragement as He was already there.

Knowing your value to God is not bound up in what you can do for Him, but in *who* you are to Him, and who He is to you.

During this first contemplative prayer time we learned so much that it encouraged us to try other ways of praying. Later on we chose to participate in *Lectio Divina*, or translating from the Latin, 'Divine Reading'. We knew the effectiveness of this depended on the willingness of all members to participate. We offered an alternate activity, such as a craft workshop or a guided walk.

Those who wanted to pray chose the area of the room they preferred and selected their floor cushions or chairs and began to settle down. We did some deep breathing exercises and tried to make ourselves quiet.

Divine Reading could be broken down into four stages:

Reading. The chosen passage was read silently, slowly, and repeated several times. Once we had understood what the passage was about, we allowed the Holy Spirit to guide us to the most important words for each of us.

Meditate. We dwelt on the words God had given us, reflecting on them, and pondering them in our hearts. We tried to let the Holy Spirit use the word or phrase to reach those parts of each one of us that needed to be healed, challenged or changed.

Oratio or *Response*. We encouraged our hearts to speak to God about the reflection we had made on His Word.

Contemplation. We rested in the Word of God and listened to His still, small voice. It was like gazing on God and feeling the need to be changed. We were going to take what we had learned and allow it to change our lives.

We selected the first four verses of Psalm 91 to read.

> Whoever dwells in the shelter of the Most High
> will rest in the shadow of the Almighty.
> I will say of the LORD, 'He is my refuge and my
> fortress,
> my God, in whom I trust.'
> Surely he will save you
> from the fowler's snare
> and from the deadly pestilence.
> He will cover you with his feathers,
> and under his wings you will find refuge;
> his faithfulness will be your shield and rampart.
> *Psalm 91:1-4*

We worked through the four stages of the *Lectio Divina* and then shared what we had read, heard and learned. The words which were most defined by the group were dwelling, shelter, rest and trust.

From meditating on the passage, people felt that the picture they received was one of intimate, tender care and protection given by God. There was a requirement stipulated by God that we dwell with Him. Talking to and listening to Him were important, as was acknowledging Him to others. We knew we were being called to know God's Word and obey it.

The reference to 'covering with his feathers' in verse 4 for one person meant the protection of a child by their father. They had no recollection of their own father, and so this picture of God with His child was particularly powerful for them.

The response to the reading was to pray out loud. They thanked God for His commitment to them. One person expressed how wonderful it felt for them to be called to dwell with God. People praised Him for His provision and care of them.

During Contemplation, some members of the group were visibly moved and tearful. One person shared God's challenge to her. She was to stop dithering, choose faith and get real with Him.

A very important truth for the group was how this psalm spoke of how we can depend on God for help and protection when life is scary. All members could identify with scary times in their own lives because of illness. This made them acknowledge that God knew what they needed and when.

In verse 4 'wings' are mentioned. One person was led to think of a prayer shawl, and as the person imagined using it, they experienced safety and refuge as they came closer to God in prayer.

Another person was amazed that it said God's faithfulness would be her 'shield' (verse 4). She had thought the shield of faith was dependent on her faith in God, and was relieved to discover that it was God's faith in her that shielded her.

On the same line a 'rampart' is mentioned. This is a defensive wall in a castle's design. As they were built to protect something precious and of value, we decided that the mention of a rampart here must mean we are protected because we are precious and valued by God.

Someone who was deeply moved said they had heard a voice say, 'I offer you Myself, now I want you to offer Me yourself.' They were encouraged to make an acceptance prayer at that time, and made themselves accountable to the group.

An older person in the group was led to a passage in Isaiah. 'Even to your old age and grey hairs I am he, I am he who will sustain you. I have made you and I will carry you; I will sustain you and I will rescue you' (Isaiah 46:4). What a beautiful message to be given and how personal that was for them.

We all found that this prayer time had brought us closer to God. By setting ourselves apart for a while from the demands of the world, we were able to discipline ourselves to listen to God's Word. We found Divine Reading a valuable and personal way of hearing from God.

We asked the group to write anonymously which gifts they recognised and valued in the meetings. The list was humbling: calm, warmth, maturity, understanding, vulnerability, generosity, gentleness, intelligence, love, caring, loyalty, reassurance, humour – this last one was mentioned many times. Indeed, who else could laugh at the extremes of the mental health spectrum than those who have suffered within it? Humour was a binding force, as we were not laughing at one individual, but rather at ourselves, or often at the absurdity of the ignorance shown by some aspects of bureaucracy or legislation that through their questions in assessing benefit claims, demonstrated a complete lack of understanding of the nature of mental ill health.

In the group we could talk about our mental health openly and freely and still count on an empathetic response; the members could lower all protective barriers. The trust we had was evident in the way that people could be vulnerable within the group and in the way those listening would share their experience of a similar problem, encourage others with information of how they had managed it, and affirm that they could too. These moments were very beautiful and reminded me that this group was God's idea. I felt truly blessed to be part of it.

We learned that kindness and respect were universal languages and could be understood no matter how ill someone was feeling. They cut through fear and pain and reached the person who suffered, so that they experienced the faithfulness and acceptance of the group, knowing they were supported through difficult symptoms and the side effects of medication. This was ongoing and unconditional love in action.

In the Mental Health Fellowship we chose topics to explore that touched the members' lives in challenging ways. Some members lived alone by choice; others had moved away from difficult home environments. Loneliness was a common problem. We participated in a workshop looking at loneliness, defining what it was, and expressing the feelings it brings. Then we developed a positive plan, researching local resources. We then found Bible verses that encouraged us. We reported back from our discussion groups and built up an information board about loneliness.

The group talked about aloneness being different from loneliness; some people choose to work alone to allow creativity to blossom. Others acknowledged it was possible to feel lonely in a crowd. Loneliness was seen as a powerful negative experience, which can be exacerbated by the lifestyles we choose. The words to describe this feeling were listed as: rejected, abandoned, insecure, anxious, sad, unloved, angry, isolated, not accepted.

Nuclear families had fewer social contacts than extended families. Moving away from family to another area for work would bring its own challenges. Circumstantial changes such as divorce, bereavement, retirement and unemployment could all increase loneliness.

Some members of the group expressed almost constant feelings of loneliness, which were unrelated to external events or any particular time of life. When they felt very low in their mood, the isolation they felt was debilitating. They would hide away in their homes. Some reported they had used telephone help lines at such times, and found them helpful.

Having collected all this information, we then devised a plan so that people could cope with being alone.

- Keeping a journal where they could express their thoughts and feelings and which would act as a record of their mood was one method chosen by some members.

- Prayer, meditation and reading God's Word was acknowledged as very helpful, but to be done when people were able, not as a compulsory activity.

- They could focus on something that interested them, so they could appreciate the pleasure it gave them, and be thankful for it.
- They could learn to be with others; to be curious about things and to ask people questions.
- They might join local interest groups, where they could talk about their interest.
- They could take classes, where all the class would be part of the learning process; this could stimulate conversation.
- Several members of the group were already volunteering in local enterprises and finding satisfaction in giving of themselves.
- The local library, newspapers and the internet could give contact information about societies, interest groups, sports and evening classes, voluntary groups and friendship clubs.
- We acknowledged that talking therapies would be helpful, and if they were not available through the NHS in Cumbria, they were available through mental health charities.

There were many verses in the Bible that referred to isolation and loneliness, and we chose those which applied most closely to the group. 'You are my hiding place; you will protect me from trouble and surround me with songs of deliverance' (Psalm 32:7). This verse helped people to remember that wherever they were and whatever situations they found themselves in, God was with them, and would protect them. 'The LORD appeared to us in the past, saying: I have loved you with an everlasting love; I have drawn you with unfailing kindness. I will build you up again' (Jeremiah 31:3-4).

These verses reassured us that our relationship with God was ongoing, and determined by His love for us. That however we felt about being lonely, God was always with us. He would stay and heal.

We challenged one another to be more proactive in choosing to get involved with groups in the community and in our church. We promised to be accountable to one another about our ongoing commitment in these groups.

I was invited to speak at a mental health day open to church leaders and members of local churches in the area. Other opportunities came to speak to leaders in parishes and to pastoral leaders and workers in other areas. From this, people came forward and asked for support when setting up mental health support in their own churches.

I have written articles in a local newspaper and in a national Christian magazine. The Lord has provided many opportunities to share this vision of increasing understanding and offering support for those with mental health issues in churches.

I have mentioned before that the Mental Health Fellowship included members who had a short-term episode of depression, recovered, and then entered fully into their lives again. But it also included those who had experienced repeated episodes of illness, which they continued to experience. All major mental health illnesses were represented at different times in the group and in an effort to increase our knowledge and understanding of each one, we would study them. For those members who felt able, they were encouraged to share valuable first-hand experience of their illness.

We took a whole person approach to mental health, sometimes called the 'spiritual model', looking at the inner identity; how a personal sense of meaning, identity and issues around community support can keep people healthy, and help them to recover health. The report from the Spiritual and Mental Health Project in 2003[10] found a sense of group identity and shared faith aided healing, and many members of the group experienced an improvement in their mental, emotional and spiritual health.

We looked at spiritual issues, particularly our relationship with God and the promises in His Word that could inspire and strengthen us. Prayer, as you will have seen, was an important element of the life of the group. We prayed for one another as well as using a selection of chosen prayers from a number of sources.

This prayer was written by the group in one of our creative workshops:

OK to Be Me

I am accepted, loved and approved of by the creator God who made heaven and earth. I am covered by the blood of the lamb, Jesus Christ, who takes away

---

[10] Spirituality and Mental Health Project, 2003, https://www.mentalhealth.org.uk/publications/spirituality-and-mental-health-update (accessed 17th January 2018).

the sins of the world. I am filled with the Holy Spirit who brings love, power and self-discipline. It is OK to be me.

'May the God of hope fill you with all joy and peace as you trust in him, so that you may overflow with hope by the power of the Holy Spirit.'
Romans 15:13

This became a prayer we used at the end of meetings and, as we all spoke this out, the affirmation received was very powerful.

We found health professionals were becoming open to the idea that the church could have a positive effect on the recovery of people with mental health issues; they were looking to send their patients who had religious beliefs to us. Dr Andrew Powell stated: 'Those receiving religiously orientated therapy sensitive to their religious beliefs score best on post-treatment measures.'[11]

Dr Powell, a psychiatrist from the Royal College of Psychiatrists, did a study in 2004 and reading this confirmed what we have found, that rather than ignoring and discouraging spiritual input into people's treatment, which some of our members had experienced, including spiritual beliefs was proven to be of immense help.

The group prospered. We held on to our vision, to be a place of safety, where we sought to affirm, encourage and love those who needed something more than Sunday

---

[11] Dr Andrew Powell, 'Mental Health and Spirituality', 2004, https://www.rcpsych.ac.uk/pdf/Andrew Powell Mental Health and Spirituality.pdf (accessed 17th January 2018).

services in church could give. We also tried to encourage our wider church to understand the needs of those with mental health issues and feel more confident in accepting them among congregations who attend the three different services held every Sunday. The Fellowship has recently closed, just short of its thirteenth year. Support in another form goes on in the church and we hope this will spread in the diocese in the future.

As I look back, the Mental Health Fellowship was quite an adventure and the leaders learned so much from being part of it. Depending on God was essential, and we were aware of His presence with us in the richly satisfying times where the group was very blessed, but even more in the challenging, unexpected times of stress and pain and anxiety, where even in spite of this He brought answers to prayer and we saw Him working His purposes out.

There have been so many changes in people who came to the group in desperate need, and who slowly grew in hope and trust and love of God and others. Pain diminishes who you are, but God restores 'the years the locusts have eaten' (see Joel 2:25-26) and gives so much of Himself that pain can be a catalyst through which you become more like Him. It is a great joy to see those people become more fully themselves, as God is calling them to be. I found that in the process of being a wounded healer, my scars have faded so that I rarely feel them.

Oasis

From the work in the Mental Health Fellowship group I became aware that the needs of carers in our communities are often unrecognised. There are 6.5 million registered carers in Britain, although charities suggest there are many more carers who do not recognise themselves as such, or do not realise they may be able to receive support for the valuable work that they do.

A carer is someone who 'cares, unpaid, for a friend or family member who, due to illness, disability, a mental health problem or an addiction, cannot cope without their support'.[12]

I met carers who came to the fellowship who were often in need of a listening ear. Some of the key problems for carers were that they could feel isolated or lonely, and not be seen as a person in their own right. They often seemed to be unaware of who to go to or how to receive help.

I began to seek contact with others who were interested in supporting carers in a faith-rich way. Two people

---

[12] Carers Trust 2015, https://carers.org (accessed 6th December 2017).

expressed interest and committed to pray and seek God's guidance. As we prayed, our vision grew and our anticipation of what God would do increased. This was a pattern I was used to by now in my faith life. God provided the desire in my heart and then provided the people who could share the vision.

Now momentum increased and a curate at my church offered to help with meetings. We held two meetings, inviting all those who were carers of those who experienced mental distress.

The meeting was well attended and we listened eagerly to what people were saying. We used different forms of information-gathering to ensure all had a way of sharing what they wanted to say. It was clear that for some, a way of meeting and sharing their experiences and problems would be valuable.

From our information, it was evident that an evening meeting would be the most helpful. I researched the best venues in the area as to their availability, and found a hotel where the manager was sympathetic and offered us a quiet area to meet.

We were also invited to speak at a meeting about mental health support in the community, and from this we were offered a grant which we used to pay for refreshments at each meeting and also to buy books that were lent to members.

We named the group 'Oasis' as that was what it was to many people. In our publicity for the group we described it as a place to meet and share concerns in a safe space for mutual support with others in a similar situation. This was open to carers of those who lived with mental distress.

The group became a welcoming place for numbers of people who shared deeply of their needs and faith. They gave and received love and encouragement, which helped them to continue in their caring role.

When those who lived with mental health issues self-harmed, or attempted suicide, they did not suffer alone. The carer and the family of that person suffered too. They all needed to grieve, to heal and recover. Listening to carers and praying with them was a valued part of what we did in the group.

Carers came face-to-face with negative responses, desperate calls for help, or repeated complaints. This brought a need of building carers up. They were doing an important job and very often without support. The question of 'who cares for the carer?' is an important one. We had good contacts with the local carers' group and encouraged carers to use their resources.

The group wrote a job description that seemed typical to them of a carer's role (see below). We used this in our talks in church services along with other information and guidance on the needs of those who care. This was well received and raised awareness of their needs. Some members of the congregations said they had not thought of themselves as carers, but now they would seek a carer's assessment and support from the local carers' association. We were delighted that our work was bearing fruit.

A carer's role:
The successful candidate will be on call twenty-four hours a day, seven days a week. The position is unpaid and no training will be given. You may receive criticism, disapproval and a lack of

appreciation from the person you care for. Others may not understand what you experience or be able to support you and the role will be of an uncertain timescale.

Would you or I willingly volunteer for this job? Does anyone reading this recognise the job description and feel they are doing it?

Prayer was a central feature of our meetings and we wrote a blessing, which we used at the end of each meeting:

May you know God's presence as you care,
Knowing that Jesus is the perfect carer,
May you be guided by Him, strengthened by Him,
Encouraged and upheld by Him.
May His love flow through you and heal and
Honour all those you care for.

This group was a joy to be part of; there was a grace and anointing which was evident at every meeting.

One aspect of the group was that many carers expressed the guilt they felt because of the ongoing distress of the people they cared for. They blamed themselves when the relationship became challenging. This area of guilt became something we studied as a group.

Guilt can be a crippling issue, but the Lord did provide for people. God knows us so well, and He knows we have a propensity to sin. Guilt is also something our enemy loves to hold over us, to help us feel disconnected from God.

In the New Testament we read, 'If we claim to be without sin, we deceive ourselves and the truth is not in us. If we confess our sins, he is faithful and just and will forgive us our sins and purify us from all unrighteousness' (1 John 1:8-9). We decided to have a time of confession, repentance and listening to God. As with the Mental Health Fellowship group, we also agreed to be accountable to one another about keeping a short account with God, and not letting the guilt build up.

On one occasion, the group wanted to take a time of contemplative prayer, so we settled down to still ourselves and open our minds, hearts and spirits to God. Some members were restful, one laughed, but another burst into tears. The tearful lady generously shared what her experience had been.

This lady was caring for her daughter who had been ill for a number of years. As she was in contemplation, she felt she had been sitting with her daughter and then Jesus came and sat between them. This picture in her mind had spoken so powerfully to her. She was released at that moment from a feeling that she was solely responsible for her daughter. The stifling feeling of carrying a huge burden was lifted. In one moment Jesus had redrawn the boundaries between her and her daughter. She now felt that there could be a new relationship between them. The lady said no one had ever done anything like that for her until now; she was deeply moved and so very grateful to Jesus.

From this time of prayer, healthy boundaries were developed between mother and daughter; the mother felt free to be a person with rights and needs of her own. She also felt empowered to apply to the local carers' charity where she received a carers' assessment and was offered several hours of home-sitting service. This freed her to enjoy some social activities and to see friends, while her daughter was in safe hands. Counselling was also offered. What a change had come about from one prayer. How amazing is our Saviour?

Some members of the group had unrealistic expectations of themselves. They expected to be able to make the person they cared for better. However, these people had long-term, complex mental health issues. Medication could help, but society had no cure. The longing of the carer for the healing of the person they loved could not change that. We found when we prayed, an acceptance of the situation would come, and a more positive seeking of professional help began.

False guilt was often identified in the group as we shared our concerns. False guilt is the oppressive burden that is not based on reality, but on the views of people who are placing their attitudes on others. So we examined whether what they were feeling was real or false guilt. If the guilt was real, we knew what to do with it. We prayed and confessed, repented and received forgiveness. But false guilt was not correctly placed. We needed to help one another to be real in our assessment of the situation and dismiss the false guilt by challenging wrong thinking. A hurting person might accuse their carer of not caring for them because they did not have the answers for all their needs. Although their expectations were irrational, the false guilt was strongly felt, and some had difficulty surrendering it to Jesus. After prayer we would say out loud that what had happened was not their fault. Words spoken are powerful, and this helped a number of people.

The difficult area of long-term medication was often discussed. The stigma attached to antidepressant treatment was unhelpful. I found even among carers there was some prejudice against antidepressants being used by those they were caring for. This was not healthy, as people who were prescribed antidepressants would be able to discern the negative attitude of their carer. We looked at the use of antidepressants and how they helped people with depression, and then we prayed and listened to God for His answer.

The Lord would speak to people individually, and then we would pool our wisdom. There were some tears as carers grew in their acceptance that God was involved in the scientific discovery and development of antidepressants, and that what He gave was always good. Carers expressed a new willingness to support treatments, and we always ended the prayer times with thanks and praise for what God provided.

Oasis provided help and support for a very special group of people. Carers do not choose their job of caring; it is presented to them by circumstance. They consider others before themselves – many found it hard to commit to a group which was for their own support. The group closed in 2016, leaving those involved with wonderful memories.

Reflections

What is the mental health situation like now, thirteen years after beginning the Mental Health Fellowship?

MIND, the national mental health charity, has issued their strategy for 2016–2021 called 'Building on change'.[13] They quote some bleak facts. The first is well known, thanks to a campaign to highlight mental health issues on billboards all over Britain. One in four people will experience a mental health problem in any given year. I have sometimes asked every fourth person in church if they will stand up, and then asked everyone to look at what one in four looks like. It is worth planning this or chaos may ensue! People are often shocked at this visual reminder that mental health issues are common and that we need to try to be aware of how we can help support those who suffer.

MIND goes on to say only 25 per cent of people with mental health problems receive support each year. Parliament cut the 2015–2016 funding allocation for mental health services in England by 8.25 per cent, which equates to almost £600m. The members of the Mental Health

---

[13] MIND England and Wales. Strategy for 2016–2021: 'Building on change'. https://www.mind.org.uk/about-us/our-strategy/ (accessed 16th January 2018).

Fellowship could identify with the limitations of the mental health services provided in our area. There are long waiting lists to see psychiatrists, and often a too-early discharge from psychiatric wards.

Indeed, the most serious concern for those in south Cumbria recently was that proposals have been made to close the local psychiatric unit in Kendal, resulting in extended travel for both patients and relatives and other visitors, to distant hospitals. The campaign to resist this closure has had some effect, but the outcome remains in the balance. The group members also reported a lack of CPNs when they were discharged, which could cause stress and lead to further illness.

The community services that were offered by government-funded agencies have now been cut following the withdrawal of government financial support in 2012. But MIND continued by saying that all was not lost. Public attitudes and knowledge of mental health problems and those who suffer were improving.

There are some indications that more understanding of the needs of relatives by health professionals are leading to new support ideas being offered. The findings are that when support is given to relatives in their caring role, this enables an improved response from the mentally ill patient.

A study has been undertaken, based at Lancaster University's Spectrum Centre, and also offered at five other sites across the country. This was a self-referral online initiative for relatives over the age of sixteen years who were caring for a family member with psychosis or bipolar disorder, and who were experiencing distress. This study used a peer support model. It sounded like any self-help support group, but was not limited to one local area. Through the website you could contact a REACT[14] (Relatives Education And Coping Toolkit) supporter who was a relative who had been trained to help other relatives involved with this project. The toolkit contained information about the illnesses, and stories and practical advice about what had helped other relatives. There was also an online forum where people could talk directly to other relatives using the site. REACT was funded by the National Institute for Health Research and Health Technology Assessment and has full NHS ethical approval.

It would be very interesting to see how this progressed and if relatives did find this project helpful. Our groups thought this could be a good way of pooling information and encouraging others. This could reduce the sense of isolation and helplessness felt by some carers.

We questioned how well the supporters would be trained, as they were key to the success of the venture. We also felt they would need supervision in their roles to increase their competence and confidence. They would need to be accountable and be able to seek guidance.

We did feel it was encouraging that medical professionals were accepting that lay people could play a valuable role in the care of carers. We were also encouraged that the need to provide for the carers was acknowledged by medical professionals. This was a significant development. Both the Mental Health

---

[14] www.reacttoolkit.co.uk (accessed 30th October 2017).

Fellowship and Oasis group members wondered if the lack of physical contact, for example not being able to shake hands or share coffee together, because there was only connection via the internet, might hinder the growth of trust or empathy. However, the initiative was considered a positive move.

We saw an improved situation in our own church; people were more willing to ask questions and become better informed. Attitudes are still changing and people are becoming more accepting and supportive of those in our church who experience mental distress.

The Mental Health Fellowship produced a list for our church, which distilled their hopes of what could be offered in terms of support. Large numbers of people with varied experience of mental illness and its treatment, which has been a mixture of good and bad, have contributed to this in the hope that it will be helpful to those who want to learn more of how they might be effective in their care.

Depression in our church community: How can we help?

- Provide a loving, warm, understanding, compassionate atmosphere of friendship and acceptance, which starts with leadership and permeates downwards.

- Don't say, 'If you were really a Christian you wouldn't be depressed.' This has been said by Christians to members of our group, but it is not true. Elijah and Job and others went through depression, which was unrelated to sin. It is possible to be God-directed and God-orientated, yet still be depressed.

- Assure them that God loves them as they are now. No striving or perfection is needed for God to accept and love them.

- Provide encouragement consistently and patiently; depression can rob you of positivity and last a long time.

- Do not be afraid of depressed people or avoid them. Be a friend. Stand alongside them.

- Pray with them, for them, and encourage them to pray. Tell them you are praying for them.

- Sympathise, empathise and listen when you can. Depression can be experienced by anyone. Much can be learned through depression, and faith can mature. Those suffering in depression can be seen as soldiers in training. Encourage them.

- Treat any doubts graciously. People who struggle with faith and question what they believed when they were well do so because they are serious in their search. Share your faith with them and keep assuring them that God heals.

- Encourage them to seek medical help. They may need you to go with them. Talking to a doctor about how you feel when you are depressed is not easy.

- If medication is prescribed, be positive in your encouragement. Four to eighteen months is the average time people need to take antidepressants. They are effective treatment for many.

- A holistic approach can be more effective, so encourage them in attending talking therapies.
- Words may not mean much to a deeply depressed person. If appropriate, touch – give a hug or a touch of a hand. They are worth many words.
- Guard their activities; be protective to reduce stress or over-busyness.
- Include them in your activities and encourage exercise.
- Enduring depression requires courage; tell them they are brave and encourage them to keep going.

When the Lord sees someone with mental distress, He sees the person as unique and incomparable. He can meet their needs without doubt or fear. He knows no stress because of the length of time they have been unwell. He accepts them with love and joy in who they are. He does not doubt they will be well in time.

We who profess a desire to be more like Jesus would do well to trust Him to enable us to see beyond the diagnostic label and seek to know the person. I believe the Lord set this in my heart, that those who experience mental distress should not have to face the accusations, condemnation and scorn of judgemental people; they should not be avoided, feared and left to their fate.

The parable of the Good Samaritan in Luke 10:25-37 tells us what Jesus would do. We are called to love our neighbour. The Lord's way is to accept, come alongside, understand, support, comfort, encourage and edify hurting people, and I believe that is what God is calling us to do for each other in our churches.

What about the future? It would be good to continue to offer support in our church, and this may of course adapt as people's requirements change. It would also be good to offer education about mental health needs in churches to increase skills and confidence in our ability to support them. I pray that we can adapt and grow in our understanding of the needs of those in our congregations who suffer mental distress, so that they are enabled to experience well-being, grow in confidence in managing their health and grow in their discipleship.

I have learned so much since my diagnosis of illness. God is very protective of His vulnerable children. He never leaves them or judges them because they are ill. He knows what is needed, and when your symptoms cause you to feel He is far away, that is when He is closer than your own breathing. You discover the strength of God's arm by leaning all your weight on it; every time you trust God more, He 'gets bigger' to you. I see in hindsight that I was enabled to get close to God as a new Christian because He was preparing me for the trauma of illness to come. You need the mountaintop experiences to resource you for the valleys, which in turn give you hunger for the mountain-top experiences. This is one way we move and grow in faith.

A leper said to Jesus, 'Lord, if you are willing, you can make me clean [or, heal me]'. Jesus said He was willing, and touched him (Luke 5:12-13). Jesus, touching a leper? The witnesses must have been shocked! What a shame-shattering moment for the man who everyone avoided and judged because he had this terrible illness. Now that he was healed, what freedom for him, and what hope for others who have known shame because of mental illness! This needs to be approached in the same way that Jesus approached the leper. Acceptance, love and care are the shame-destroying gifts we have the power to give to those who struggle with mental distress.

A Final Word

While this book has focused on the ways I have sought to support people with mental health needs in my particular situation, there will be other ways that you may find helpful. I pray that my experiences can encourage you to seek God for those in your churches and communities who need mental health support.

I would be happy to hear from anyone who has questions or ideas about mental health support, or who would appreciate sharing experiences. Do email me at: lorraine@gibbard.myzen.co.uk

Resources

The Mental Health Fellowship had a resource library that members of the group used. These were our most valued books and most often-read.

Anderson, Neil T and Joanne, *Overcoming Depression* (Bloomington, MN: Bethany House Publishers, 2004).

Baker, Barbara, *When Someone You Love Has Depression* (London: Sheldon Press, 2003). A practical help for carers.

Johnstone, Matthew, *I Had a Black Dog* (Sydney, Australia: Pan, 2005). Also found on YouTube: www.youtube.com (World Health Organization); www.blackdoginstitute.org.au (accessed 29th November 2017).

Johnstone, Matthew and Ainsley Johnstone, *Living With a Black Dog* (London: Robinson, 2009).

Ledger, Chris, and Wendy Bray, *Insight Into Depression* (Surrey: CWR, 2009).

Lockley, John, *A Practical Workbook for the Depressed Christian* (Milton Keynes: Authentic, 2002).

Murray, David, *Christians Get Depressed Too* (Grand Rapids, MI: Reformation Heritage Books, 2010).

Swinney, Joanna, *Through the Dark Woods* (Oxford: Lion Hudson, 2006).

Williams, Chris, Paul Richards and Ingrid Whitton, *I'm Not Supposed to Feel Like This* (London: Hodder & Stoughton, 2002).

Other resources we have found helpful:

Local

BORDERLINE. Counselling Services
42a Warwick Road, Carlisle CA1 1DN
Tel: 01228 596900
Email: info@borderlinecounselling.co.uk
Website: www.borderlinecounselling.co.uk

FIRST STEP. NHS Psychological Therapies
Access through GP or self-referral
The Hub, Elmwood, Tynefield Drive, Penrith, CA11 8JA
Tel: 0300 123 9122
Website. www.cumbriapartnership.nhs.uk

GROWING WELL. Mental health support to increase confidence and learn new skills in an agricultural setting. Courses and qualifications.

Low Sizergh Farm, Kendal, LA8 8AE
Tel: 01539 61777
Email: info@growingwell.co.uk
www.growingwell.co.uk

MENTAL HEALTH FELLOWSHIP
Self-help support group
St Thomas Church, Stricklandgate, Kendal, LA9 4QG
Contact: Lorraine Gibbard
(Note: Although the Mental Health Fellowship ended recently, I continue to support individuals in church in need of mental health support, and will be working to promote mental health support in churches.)

SOUTH LAKELAND CARERS. Supporting people of any age with caring responsibilities. Carers' assessment, enabling you to access further support.
Unit 16, Shap Road Industrial Estate, Shap Road, Kendal LA9 6NZ
Tel: 01539 815970
Email: admin@slcarers.org.uk
http://slcarers.org.uk

SOUTH LAKELAND MIND. Walks, visits, drop-in service. Listening, advocacy
Kendal branch. Stricklandgate House, 92 Stricklandgate, Kendal, Cumbria LA9 4PU
Tel: 01539 740591
Email: info@slmind.org
www.slmind.org

National

BIPOLAR UK. Supporting people affected by bipolar. Help and support for carers too.
Tel: 0333 323 3880
Email: info@bipolaruk.org
Website: www.bipolaruk.org

MIND England and Wales. Provides information and support. Publications. Mind Infoline.
Tel: 0300 123 3393
Email: publications@mind.org.uk
Website: www.mind.org.uk

MENTAL HEALTH RESEARCH NETWORK
Works with parents and siblings and other carers to improve care of those with mental health issues.
Website: https://www.makingresearchbetter.co.uk/clinical -research/mental-health/

MIND AND SOUL. Exploring Christianity and mental health. Resources, support, podcasts, blogs, events, courses.
Websites: www.mindandsoulfoundation

PREMIER LIFELINE. A caring, confidential Christian helpline offering support and prayer.
Open 9am–midnight, seven days a week.
Tel: 0300 111 0101

SANELINE. Confidential helpline to listen, give information and put you in touch with services in your area. 6pm–11pm
Tel: 020 3805 1790
Email: info@sane.org.uk

RETHINK MENTAL ILLNESS. Offers advice and information on all mental health issues. There are 150 support groups across the UK. Offers support to carers, family and friends.
Website: www.rethink.org

RETHINK SIBLINGS NETWORK. Support for families. Support groups, Rethink talk forum. Your voice magazine online.
www.rethink.org/siblings

ROYAL COLLEGE OF PSYCHIATRISTS. Mental health information.
www.rcpsych.ac.uk/mentalhealthinformation.aspx

NATIONAL HEALTH INFORMATION.
www.patient.co.uk